'Round the world cooking library

British and Irish Cooking

Traditional dishes prepared in a modern way

Recipe contributions by Sally Morris,
British home economist and food consultant, London

DAVID & CHARLES : NEWTON ABBOT

Contents

0 7153 6239 9

Produced by Plenary Publications International, Inc., New York, Amsterdam Office, in the Netherlands for David & Charles (Holdings) Limited
South Devon House – Newton Abbot – Devon

Cup measures in this book are based on an eight ounce cup.

Eating with the English

In Kent, you can see the sturdy tower steeples. Here the hops for brewing beer are dried.

Fish and chips can be served either wrapped in yesterday's newspaper or in a restaurant.

Sometimes the food served in English pubs is quite elaborate.

Forthrightness and simplicity are the great strengths of cooking in the British Isles. While cooks in other countries rely on garlic and spices to enliven their food, the British approach lets the ingredients and the care of the cook speak for themselves. Vacationers returning from abroad have popularized many foreign dishes in Britain, and some people have an unjustified inferiority complex about their own traditional national cooking. But anyone who has had a superb English meal – for instance, Whitstable oysters, followed by a roast saddle of Southdown lamb, a Stilton cheese with a glass of port and walnuts – can testify to the glories of British cooking. And above all, those grand traditional pillars of English cuisine – breakfast and high tea – are unsurpassed anywhere in the world.
Alas, though, these age-old traditions are slowly crumbling, especially in the cities. There are two obvious reasons: lack of

Restaurants in London are as elegant as anywhere in the world.

In the winter, hot chestnuts are sold in the streets of London.

time and fear of calories. Hardly anyone facing a long ride to work in the morning can find the time to enjoy a cooked breakfast at his leisure, and any weight watcher can only view with a suspicious eye bacon and eggs, sausages and porridge in the morning; all sorts of pies and pastries, scones, buns and muffins at five in the afternoon.
Although this undoubtedly holds true for the majority of city dwellers, in the country (and the typical Englishman has always preferred country life to city life) you can still encounter the genuine breakfast and high tea rituals, especially in Scotland, where the pace of life is less hectic and the bracing climate requires substantial meals.
Mrs. Eliza Acton, author of a famous Victorian cookbook, wrote that among the aristocracy roasted partridge or pigeons under silver covers for breakfast were not uncommon. Today we won't find those even at a ducal castle. Yet arriving from abroad, anyone staying at a good English country hotel might still rub his eyes in disbelief at the breakfast table. To begin with there is a choice of fried eggs, eggs 'sunny-side-up', ham and eggs, bacon and eggs, scrambled eggs with sausages and grilled tomatoes, fried kidneys, and smoked fish such as the famed kipper and the Finnan Haddock (discovered by chance, when after a fire in the small fishing village of Findon near Aberdeen, all the salted haddock was smoked by accident).
Then of course there is the porridge, oatmeal cooked in water and traditionally eaten with salt, and just help yourself when it comes to covering it with plenty of fresh cream, or to choosing stewed fruits, such as prunes, apricots or apples. And warm, buttered toast with tart orange marmalade left to mature in old whisky vats to get its true flavor. To go with it all is the ever-present enormous pot of strong tea.
The national ritual of 'high tea' is no less daunting. It can be a housewife's chore, and since more and more wives are taking jobs, high tea is going the way of the breakfast in many places. In order to enjoy it in its full glory, here again you must visit the countryside. There may be at least two brands of tea: Chinese, Ceylon or Indian. Like tea at breakfast, these, too, should be strong and drunk with cream and sugar. There are great piles of ham, cheese, cucumber, cold chicken and water-cress sandwiches – a substantial meal, which is often eaten now instead of a later dinner.
The sandwich, in fact, is an English invention and owes its name to John Montagu, Earl of Sandwich, who lived from 1718 to 1792 and was such a passionate card player that he did not allow himself time out to eat. His solicitous butler, therefore, served him a large plateful of sliced meat and fish, each slice put between two thin pieces of bread, which the Earl could put in his mouth without having to leave his card table.
On the tea table there will also be an assortment of pies with sweet as well as 'savory' fillings, apple pie, gooseberry tarts, fruitcakes and all those delicious little goodies that only English and Scottish housewives know the secrets of: muffins, scones, crumpets and buns. Put on the end of a long fork, they are often held over an open fire to toast, and are then covered with fresh, melting butter and strawberry jam.
Until recently, store-bought essentials for a high tea were regarded as an insult to good taste. Pies, cakes, muffins, scones and all the other items adorning the tea table had to be homemade, including the marmalade and jam. The English housewife has always taken a great deal of pride in the arts of baking and jam making, and in old English cookbooks there are whole series of recipes for all sorts of preserves, marmalades, jams and jellies, to which a dash of brandy or rum was often added to give it that extra flavor.
Lamb has always been a welcome dish on the English dinner table. Both leg of lamb

OATS
SPAIN

Small fishing ports lie hidden in the bays and creeks of Cornwall. The boats rise and fall with the swelling and sinking of the tide.

For many Englishmen, the climax of a vacation is the salmon fishing in Scotland. Clear sparkling streams, full of jumping salmon, still rush through the rugged Scottish mountains. Smoked salmon from Scotland is one of the delicacies most valued in Europe today.

and cold mutton are among the most traditional of meat courses. The carving of a large piece of meat is considered a high art, which is mastered to perfection by a small number of professional carvers. The most celebrated carver in all England is to be found in London's unique Simpson's-in-the-Strand There the proud carver slowly walks around the dining room in his white suit with the tall white chef's cap, pushing an enormous, beautifully decorated silver 'dome' on a trolley. When the dome is removed there is a whole leg of lamb or an enormous piece of roast beef, from which with his huge knife the carver will cut some pink, thick slices right at your table. Every part of England has its own speciality whose fame, even in this era of prepackaged, frozen convenience foods, has not yet paled. Take for instance the case of two famous creams. Devonshire and Cornwall each claim that their native cream is superior to the other's (not to

At low tide fishermen have to travel for miles across the sand to reach the shallow water.

After the salmon is smoked it is sliced thinly.

mention cream made anywhere else) and the issue has never been settled. No one will deny, though, that the two creams are delicious: thick lumpy creams, 'clotted creams' as the English call them, with their out-of-this-world flavor as they cover the first fresh strawberries of the year.

'Dover-soles' also enjoy a great reputation – those huge, white soles which usually are served grilled, but in Devon are allowed to simmer gently in that famous fresh Devonshire cream. And if a sole is designated 'Dover' on a menu it must be indeed the 'genuine article.'

Still very special treats, however, are Scottish and Irish salmon. Towards Christmas a smoked salmon can be ordered whole from Scotland or Ireland – mighty salmons caught in icy rushing rivers, their golden and silver hued smoked skins enclosing the tender meaty fish.

Many traditional English dishes are associated with Christmas – turkey with chestnut stuffing, plump roast goose, the plum pudding that the whole family takes turns stirring, and mince pies. The most ancient of all Christmas dishes is the boar's head, beautifully decorated and carefully seasoned, which forms the grand centerpiece of the festive table. Carried in procession into the royal presence at a King's feast, it must have been a monumental sight.

The most legendary Scottish dish can only be haggis. In its strictest and oldest form, haggis is a sheep's stomach turned inside out and stuffed with cooked, diced sheep's liver and oatmeal. At castles in the Highlands, the haggis is solemnly brought into the dining room, preceeded by a bagpipe player who walks around the table three times, blowing on his bagpipes, as the haggis is being carved. He departs after being rewarded with a glass of whisky, leaving the host and his guests to enjoy their haggis, which is best washed down with plenty of whisky.
A Welsh specialty is a unique sort of pancake prepared on a long-handled, round, flat iron over an open fire. There is an endless variety in these 'griddlecakes' or 'girdle cakes' and every farmer's wife cooks them in her own special way. The sea is also a good provider, and the Welsh, like all coastal people, make good use of an abundance of shellfish, and even seaweed.
Irish cuisine is far from elaborate, for Ireland, after all, has long been a poor country. But whoever delights in simplicity will all the more appreciate its superb quality. Ireland boasts delicious fresh salmon and other fish, excellent lamb dishes and the best bacon that can go with eggs. The potato is a staple part of the diet, and – according to the Irish themselves – no one masters the art of boiling potatoes as well as they do. But there is one Irish dish all foreigners need a while to warm up to – Carrageen Moss, a kind of seaweed made into a sweet jelly by adding milk and lemon juice.

The English pub is an institution unique in the whole world. Typical of the many pubs in London is the Waterman's Arms.

A distillery is nestled between the hills in the Western isles of Scotland.

The barley is tossed from time to time as it germinates.

Part of the pleasure of playing cricket is the anticipation of a beer at the end of the game.

Scotsmen discuss their whisky.

Beverages

The picturesque inns also belong to the charm of the English countryside. These centuries-old public houses often played very important roles in English history Secret meetings were frequently arranged between the politicians, writers and military men who lodged there. Occasionally a small inn owes its fame to the fact that this was the meeting place for a King and his first love.

England's principal brew is beer, and the country has an endless variety from the light or mild 'ale' to the heavy, dark 'stout.' The Englishman likes to drink his beer in a 'pub,' the typically English public house or 'local' where the whole neighborhood gets together, standing at the bar discussing the topics of the day, or playing darts or skittles. The typically English pub is treated as almost a club by its 'regulars,' and it is the best place to meet the English often 'at their best behavior.' Many pubs are very picturesque, some of them centuries old with local traditions and the most outlandish collection of prints, ships' models, tankards, old newspapers and what-have-you's.

Although vineyards are rare in Britain (the grape was brought by Romans but after Henry VIII abolished the monasteries their great vineyards wasted away) the English are taken to be experienced judges of wine. 'In France they can make wine, in England they can drink it,' is a saying that contains a good deal of truth. As the region around Bordeaux was occupied by the English for almost three centuries during the Middle Ages, the people of England have become great Bordeaux drinkers, and Bordeaux wine in Britain is still called by its medieval French name 'claret.' German wines were introduced to England by Queen Victoria,

ORKNEY ISLES
SCOTLAND
ABERDEEN
NORTH SEA
DUNDEE
ATLANTIC OCEAN
GLASGOW
EDINBURG
ULSTER
BELFAST
MAN
YORKSHIRE
IRISH SEA
LIVERPOOL
MANCHESTER
DUBLIN
DERBYSHIRE
CHESHIRE
EIRE
STAFFORDSHIRE
BIRMINGHAM
HUNTINGDON-SHIRE
WALES
ENGLAND
LONDON
SOMERSET
DOVER
SUSSEX
DEVONSHIRE
CORNWALL
THE CHANNEL

who developed her taste from her German husband Prince Albert.

The most popular English apéritif is sherry, a wine from southern Spain, introduced to England by Sir Francis Drake, the dauntless seaman who was one of the favorites of Queen Elizabeth I. For his queen he had captured the Spanish town of Cadiz and loaded his ships with the golden wines from nearby Jerez. The drink became so popular with the English that it has virtually become their national wine, under the name of sherry, which is nothing more or less than a corrupted pronunciation of the Spanish name 'Jerez'.

England's favorite after-dinner wine is port, first brought to Britain from Portugal in the 17th century. An old bottle of port should be covered with dust, and to drink port in England is to be surrounded with time-honored rites: a gentleman never leaves the serving of port to his butler but will always pour it himself, and never from the bottle, but always from a decanter. In former days the firstborn son of a wealthy family was presented with 144 bottles of port of the year of his birth and they were left to age in the cellar until the child had grown to adulthood. Twenty-one years later the port was considered mature enough to be drunk, and the young man old enough to drink it. Port should always be served after dinner, mostly with cheese and biscuits, or with dessert, fruits and nuts. And in old-fashioned families ladies are expected to depart from the dining room when the port decanter is brought to the table.

Although England produces almost no wine from grapes, it does have an excellent apple wine, strong cider, primarily from Cornwall, Devonshire and Somerset. Moreover, in rural England homemade wines are increasingly popular, especially those made from raspberries, blackberries, rhubarb and dandelions. The inhabitants of a cold and damp country like England are, of course, very fond of beverages with a high alcohol content. Great Britain is still France's top consumer when it comes to French cognac.

Gin, however, has been distilled in England for centuries. It seems that English mercenary troops who fought in the Netherlands in the 17th century took the Dutch 'jenever', made from juniper berries, as a happy means of reconciling themselves to the penetrating damp cold of the Dutch winter. Presumably, it was they who introduced the distillation of gin in England, where for a long time it was the drink of coachmen, charwomen, sailors and street vendors. A gentleman wouldn't dream of touching it.

But when the Royal Navy gave gin 'snob-appeal' by combining gin and angostura bitters as an officer's drink (pink gin) and after the First World War when the cocktail fashion blew over from the United States and especially the dry Martini found favor with the English, 'respectability' opened its doors to gin and today no Englishman is embarrassed at the sight or taste of gin. Both gin-and-it (Italian vermouth) and gin-and-tonic are now very popular with the ladies.

Whisky, too, shows a similar development. In the last century whisky was still regarded by many as a drink for poor Irish peasants and tough Scottish Highlanders. If he wanted something more potent than wine, an English gentleman would turn to French cognac. But whisky's incomparable qualities were finally appreciated and whisky has become more or less the national English 'spirit', although the Scots disdainfully look down their noses at the way the English take their whisky, with plenty of sodawater and (even!) ice. A Scot won't be caught dead drinking his whisky like that: no ice because according to the Scots, it kills the delicate flavor of the whisky ('Scotch-on-the-rocks' is a dirty word in Scotland), and *no* sodawater; a shot of plain water at the utmost, from a fresh Scottish brook and not from a city's kitchen faucet.

Most Scotch that reaches America is a blend of whiskies from various parts of Scotland. Every Highland valley (or 'glen' as it is called) has its own particular whisky, its taste depending on the water, the quality of the turf above which the grain is dried (the smoke of the turf gives the whisky its typical 'dried cork' taste) and also on the local malt and barley. For whisky to be proper whisky it must be left to age for at least eight years in wooden vats, preferably old sherry barrels. This maturing process gives the whisky its golden color and warm, mild flavor.

And not to be forgotten is Irish whiskey, distilled in a unique way to give it a somewhat heavier aroma. A very fashionable drink is Irish Coffee, which consists of a shot of Irish whiskey, brown sugar and hot coffee. This mixture is stirred before adding, very carefully, over the back of a spoon, a generous amount of not-too-whipped cream and then drunk by sipping the hot coffee through the cream floating on top. And, as the observant reader may already have noticed, the Irish drink is spelled with an 'e' (whiskey), the Scottish variety without the 'e' (whisky).

Cheeses

The Cutty Sark, now lies still forever in the Thames. She was the last of the famous 'clipper ships' carrying cargoes of tea or wool.

Stilton is known as the 'king of cheeses.' It is traditionally served with a glass of port.

Anyone who wants to get acquainted with the delightful variety of English cheeses can see them all together in the world-famous little cheese shop on Jermyn Street in London's fashionable St. James's. They are displayed there in all their golden richness, each traditional English cheese with its own particular spicy, creamy or pungent flavor. The English are probably the world's greatest cheese lovers, and after lunch or dinner they like to have their cheese with dry biscuits while enjoying a glass of port.

Caerphilly – a flat cheese, originally made in the Welsh village of Caerphilly but today also produced in Somerset. A pleasant, mild cheese with a taste slightly reminiscent of buttermilk.

Cheddar – the most imitated of all English cheeses, produced in North America, Australia and New Zealand, and now even France. Almost anywhere cows graze today you can be sure 'Cheddar' is being manufactured. But it only vaguely resembles the genuine English farmhouse Cheddar which, in fact, is difficult to come by even in Britain. Genuine farmhouse Cheddar is made of milk from a particular farm where cows graze in particular pastures. There must be as many different farmhouse Cheddars as French wines.

Cheshire – a family of large, tall cheeses that come in several varieties: white Cheshire, actually a light yellow, 'red' Cheshire, artificially colored to a deep orange, and a blue-green, veined variety, the so-called 'blue' Cheshire.

Wensleydale – a cheese from Yorkshire, usually white with a mild, rich, milky flavor. There is also a rare blue-veined variety, a delicacy not readily available.

Derby – a mild cheese from Derbyshire, rather neutral without a sharp flavor of its own, which is why finely chopped sage is often added, giving the soft yellow cheese its light green 'clouds.'

Stilton – the most famous, and according to many, the finest of all English cheeses comes from Huntingdonshire. It is a tall cheese, creamily textured with greenish-blue mildewed veins and the best cheese to go with a glass of port at the end of a meal. In fact, so admired is the Stilton and port combination that the two are blended together and sold in earthenware jars at London's choicest shops.

Covent Garden is not only famous as a vegetable market in London, but it is also the name of a famous opera and ballet theater. The market and the theater stand side by side.

Home-made cakes are sold in small shops throughout England, Scotland and Wales.
A small farmhouse in Wales reflects the peoples' love of music, poetry and literature.

A breed of shaggy long-haired cattle graze among the grasses of Scotland. This is a hefty beef race with woolly hide and long horns. They give particularly good meat and exceptionally fine steaks.

Soups

Hotch potch

Lamb and vegetable soup

8 servings

1½ pounds stewing lamb with bones
½ cup flour seasoned with ¾ teaspoon salt
Freshly ground black pepper
2 tablespoons oil
8 cups cold water
2 onions, finely chopped
2 carrots, finely chopped
1 small turnip, diced
½ small cauliflower, separated into flowerets
½ cup lima beans, fresh or frozen
½ cups peas, fresh or frozen
1 cup lettuce leaves, shredded
2 tablespoons, finely chopped parsley

Roll pieces of lamb in flour seasoned with salt and pepper. Sauté the meat in the oil until lightly browned. Place the lamb in a large saucepan and cover with cold water. Cover saucepan and simmer for 1½ hours.
Add all the vegetables except the lettuce and peas. Simmer vegetables for 25 minutes.
Add lettuce and peas and simmer another 10 minutes. Remove lamb. Discard the bones and shred meat into small pieces. Return meat to the saucepan and simmer 5 minutes. Add parsley and serve hot.
This is a summer soup, which makes use of tender, young vegetables. It should be very thick.

Scotch broth

6 servings

2 pounds stewing lamb, with bones
6 cups cold water
3 tablespoons barley, washed
2 onions, finely chopped
2 carrots, diced
2 stalks celery, diced
1 bay leaf
½ teaspoon thyme
3 tablespoons finely chopped parsley
½ teaspoon salt
Freshly ground black pepper

Place the lamb in a large casserole. Cover with cold water. Cover casserole and simmer for 1 hour. Add remaining ingedients and simmer for 1 more hour. Discard bay leaf. Remove lamb. Separate meat from the bones. Discard the bones and shred meat into small pieces. Return meat to the saucepan. Simmer for 5 more minutes.

Oxtail soup

6 servings

1 (3½ pound) oxtail, cut into 2 inch joints
½ cup flour
2 tablespoons vegetable oil
2 onions, finely chopped
2 carrots, sliced
2 stalks celery, sliced
6 cups beef broth
1 bay leaf
¼ teaspoon thyme
½ teaspoon salt
½ teaspoon peppercorns
1 tablespoon finely chopped parsley
3 cloves
⅛ teaspoon nutmeg

Garnish:
1 carrot, diced
1 small onion, cut into slices and separated into rings
1 teaspoon lemon juice
1 tablespoon Worcestershire sauce

Place oxtail joints in a large saucepan. Cover with cold water. Bring water to a boil and simmer for 10 minutes. Drain oxtail and dry the joints on paper towels. Roll joints in flour. Brown oxtail in hot oil. Add onions, carrots and celery and continue cooking for 5 minutes. Add broth, bay leaf, thyme, salt, peppercorns, parsley, cloves and nutmeg. Cover and simmer over low heat for 3 hours until meat is tender. Remove joints and strip off all the meat. Strain the broth and chill for 4 hours. Remove fat from the broth. Cook diced carrot and onion in simmering broth for 15 minutes. Add meat from oxtails. Add lemon juice and Worcestershire sauce. Simmer 5 minutes and serve hot.

Mulligatawny

Curry soup

8 servings

- 1¼ *pounds chicken or ½ a 3 pound chicken cut into serving pieces*
- 4 *cups beef broth*
- 1 *onion, sliced*
- 1 *carrot, sliced*
- 1 *stalk celery, sliced*
- ½ *teaspoon salt*
- 2 *tablespoons butter*
- 1 *onion, finely chopped*
- 1 *green apple, peeled, cored and sliced*
- 1 *tablespoon curry powder*
- 2 *tablespoons flour*
- 1 *bay leaf*
- ¼ *teaspoon allspice*
- ¼ *cup heavy cream*

Place the chicken in a casserole. Add beef broth, onion, carrot, celery and salt. Cover and simmer for 1 hour. Remove chicken. Discard the skin and bones and cut chicken meat into small pieces. Strain the broth. Chill for 4 hours and remove fat which will have risen to the surface. In a saucepan, heat the butter and cook the chopped onion and apple together for 3 minutes. Stir in curry powder and flour and cook for 1 minute. Add broth, bay leaf and allspice. Cover and simmer 15 minutes. Add chicken pieces and cream and continue cooking for 5 minutes until chicken is hot.

It is customary to serve a small separate bowl of hot boiled rice with Mulligatawny soup.

Cock-a-leekie

Chicken soup with leeks

8 servings

- 1 *(1½ pound) chicken*
- 6 *cups water*
- 2 *tablespoons butter*
- 6 *leeks, sliced or 2 cups scallions, white and green part, chopped*
- 1 *teaspoon salt*
- *Freshly ground black pepper*
- 2 *tablespoons finely chopped parsley*

Place chicken in a large pot. Add water and simmer for 1 hour until chicken is tender. Slice chicken into thin strips. Chill the chicken broth for 4 hours and remove fat which will have risen to the surface. Melt the butter. Add leeks or scallions, salt and pepper. Cover and simmer over low heat for 15 minutes until soft and tender. Add chicken broth and chicken. Simmer another 10 minutes and garnish with parsley.

Feather fowlie

Chicken soup with ham

8 servings

- 1 *(2½ pound) chicken*
- 1 *(12 ounce) slice smoked ham or boiled ham in 1 piece*
- 2 *onions, chopped*
- 2 *stalks celery, chopped*
- 1 *carrot, sliced*
- 4 *tablespoons finely chopped parsley*
- ¼ *teaspoon thyme*
- ⅛ *teaspoon nutmeg*
- 7 *cups water*
- 1 *teaspoon salt*
- *Freshly ground black pepper*
- 3 *egg yolks*
- ½ *cup heavy cream*

Place the chicken in a heavy casserole. Add ham, onions, celery, carrot, 2 tablespoons parsley, thyme, nutmeg, water, salt and pepper. Bring to simmering point. Cover the pan and simmer over low heat for 1 hour. Remove chicken from the carcass and cut into very small pieces. Remove ham from casserole and cut into small pieces. Return the chicken carcass to the pan and simmer for 1 more hour.

Strain the broth. Cool and then chill in the refrigerator for 4 hours. Skim fat from the broth. Return broth to simmering point and add chicken and ham. Combine eggs and cream.

Add to hot soup. Heat until cream is hot but do not allow soup to boil. Garnish with remaining 2 tablespoons of parsley.

Leek and potato soup

6 servings

- 4 *cups chicken broth*
- ½ *teaspoon salt*
- 4 *medium sized all purpose potatoes, diced*
- 3 *yellow onions, chopped*
- 3 *leeks, white part only, chopped or 1 additional onion*
- ½ *teaspoon chervil*
- 2 *tablespoons finely chopped parsley*
- ½ *cup heavy cream*
- 1 *tablespoon butter*

Bring broth to simmering point. Add the salt, potatoes, onions and leeks. Cover the pan and simmer for 20 minutes. Partially mash the potatoes into the broth with a potato masher. (Do not mash the potatoes and onions completely but leave them in small recognizable pieces.) Add chervil, parsley, cream and butter. Simmer uncovered for 3 minutes until cream is hot.

Note: To make a thick cream soup, place all the ingredients, except the parsley, in a blender when the soup has been completed. Garnish the soup with parsley.

Watercress soup

4 servings

1 bunch watercress
2 tablespoons butter
1 onion, finely chopped
1 stalk celery, chopped
2 medium sized potatoes, cubed
3 cups chicken broth, simmering
1 tablespoon lemon juice
½ teaspoon salt
Freshly ground black pepper
½ cup heavy cream

Wash watercress. Reserve ½ cup of the leaves. Chop remaining leaves and stems into small pieces. Melt the butter in a saucepan and sauté onion and celery for 3 minutes. Add the watercress, potatoes, broth, lemon juice, salt and pepper. Cover and simmer for 30 minutes. Purée the soup in a blender. Strain blended soup and return to a clean saucepan. Add cream and heat to simmering point. Add reserved watercress leaves and serve hot or cold.

Cullen skink

Haddock and potato soup

6 servings

1 pound smoked haddock or other smoked salt water fish
2½ cups cold water
½ teaspoon salt
3 medium sized potatoes, cut into quarters
1 onion, chopped
4 cups milk, simmering
⅛ teaspoon nutmeg
Freshly ground black pepper
2 tablespoons finely chopped parsley
6 slices freshly made toast

Place the fish in a saucepan and add the cold water. Bring to simmering point and add salt, potatoes and onion. Cover and simmer for 25 minutes. Drain fish and potatoes and place in a blender. Add 1 cup of milk and turn on the motor. Blend until smooth. Add soup to the remaining simmering milk. Season with nutmeg and pepper. Stir over low heat for 5 minutes. Garnish with parsley. Serve hot with freshly made toast.

Lentil soup

6 servings

1¼ cups lentils
4 strips bacon
2 onions, finely chopped
2 carrots, chopped
2 stalks celery, chopped
5 cups water
1 bay leaf
3 sprigs parsley
½ teaspoon thyme
1 teaspoon salt
Freshly ground black pepper
1 teaspoon tomato paste
½ cup boiled ham, diced

Wash lentils several times in cold water, then soak in cold water 2 hours. Drain the lentils. Fry the bacon until crisp. Drain on paper towels and discard all but 2 tablespoons of bacon fat. Fry onions, carrots and celery in bacon fat for 5 minutes. Transfer to a saucepan and add drained lentils, 5 cups water, bacon, bay leaf, parsley, thyme, salt pepper and tomato paste. Cover and simmer over low heat for 1½ hours. Purée the soup in a blender. Strain the soup and return to a clean saucepan. (Add ½ cup additional water or chicken broth if the soup is too thick. This depends on the type of lentils used.) Return soup to simmering point and garnish with diced ham. Serve hot.

Green pea soup

6 servings

½ pound dried split peas
5 cups chicken broth
2 tablespoons butter
2 onions, finely chopped
1 carrot, chopped
2 stalks celery, chopped
1 teaspoon sugar
1 teaspoon dried mint
½ teaspoon salt
Freshly ground black pepper
½ cup heavy cream
3 slices bread, cut into croutons
3 tablespoons butter or oil

Wash the peas. Place in a bowl, cover with cold water and soak for 8 hours. Drain and rinse the peas.
Place the peas in a saucepan. Add chicken broth. Bring to simmering point over low heat. Cover and cook for 1 hour until peas are tender. Heat the butter and sauté onions, carrot and celery for 5 minutes. Add to saucepan with peas. Add sugar, mint, salt and pepper and continue cooking for 20 minutes. Pureé the soup in a blender. Strain into a clean saucepan. Add the cream and heat 2 minutes until cream is hot.
Fry croutons in hot butter or oil. Drain on paper towels. Garnish pea soup with croutons.

Fish dishes

Old English baked cod

4 servings

- *4 (6 ounce) cod-fish steaks*
- *2 tablespoons butter*
- *1 onion, finely chopped*
- *4 mushrooms, finely chopped*
- *3 tablespoons finely chopped parsley*
- *¼ teaspoon thyme*
- *1 bay leaf*
- *½ teaspoon salt*
- *Freshly ground black pepper*
- *2 cups milk*
- *1½ tablespoons cornflour dissolved in 2 tablespoons cold water*
- *½ cup breadcrumbs*
- *4 strips bacon, fried until crisp*
- *4 lemon wedges*
- *Watercress or parsley for garnish*

Heat the butter in a skillet. Sauté onions and mushrooms 5 minutes. Transfer to a baking dish. Arrange cod over the mixture and add parsley, thyme, bay leaf, salt, pepper and milk. Cover dish with foil and bake in a 350° oven for 20 minutes. Remove the fish and keep it warm. Strain milk into a saucepan. Bring milk to simmering point and stir in cornflour paste. Cook 2 minutes to thicken into a sauce. Arrange cod on a clean baking dish. Cover with sauce. Top with breadcrumbs and crumbled bacon. Place under the grill for 3 minutes until crumbs are lightly browned. Garnish dish with lemon wedges and watercress or parsley.

Flounder poached in cider

6 servings

- *2 pounds flounder, filleted*
- *1 teaspoon butter*
- *4 scallions, finely chopped*
- *½ teaspoon salt*
- *Freshly ground black pepper*
- *1 cup cider*
- *2 tablespoons apple brandy*
- *1 tablespoon lemon juice*
- *2 tablespoons butter*
- *2 tablespoons flour*
- *⅓ cup heavy cream*
- *4 tablespoons Parmesan cheese, freshly grated*

Butter a baking dish and sprinkle dish with scallions. Arrange flounder fillets in a single layer in the dish. Season fish with salt and pepper. Add cider, apple brandy and lemon juice. Cover dish with aluminum foil. Place dish in a 350° oven and poach fish for 12 minutes. Strain off the liquid carefully. Keep the fish warm. Melt the butter. Stir in the flour and cook for 1 minute. Add strained liquid and cream. Pour sauce back over the fish. Sprinkle with cheese and brown under the grill for 3 minutes.

Finnan haddie is a traditional dish originating on the east coast of Scotland in Kincardineshire. For generations the Scots smoked the haddock over seaweed, though now pine and oak chips are more commonly used. Finnan haddie is frequently served topped with either a pat of butter or a poached egg. It is always accompanied by large quantities of brown bread and butter.

Finnan haddie

Poached smoked haddock

4 servings

- *1 small onion, sliced thinly*
- *1½ pounds smoked haddock*
- *2 cups milk*
- *1 bay leaf*

Sauce:

- *2 tablespoons butter*
- *2 tablespoons flour*
- *1 teaspoon prepared (Dijon type) mustard*
- *2 tablespoons finely chopped parsley*

Place onion slices in a shallow buttered baking dish. Lay fish on the onion and add milk and bay leaf. Cover dish with aluminum foil and poach the fish in a 350° oven for 15 minutes. Remove fish and keep it warm. Strain and reserve poaching liquid. To prepare the sauce, heat the butter in a small saucepan. Stir in the flour and cook for 1 minute. Add reserved poaching liquid. Stir constantly until a medium thick sauce is formed. Stir in mustard and parsley. Serve the sauce separately.

Lobster salad

4 servings

- *3 (1½ pound) lobsters*
- *1 lettuce*
- *2 medium sized ripe tomatoes, sliced*
- *1 small cucumber, sliced*
- *2 hard boiled eggs, sliced*
- *12 black olives, pitted*
- *1 cup mayonnaise*
- *½ teaspoon finely chopped parsley*
- *¼ teaspoon tarragon*
- *1 teaspoon chives*

Boil the lobsters for 18 minutes. Remove the lobster meat. Cut the meat into small pieces and reserve the coral (if you have selected lady lobsters). Wash the lettuce and arrange the leaves on a large platter. Arrange alternating slices of tomato, cucumber and egg around the edge of the platter. Decorate the platter with black olives. Arrange the lobster in the center of the platter. Combine the mayonnaise with the herbs. Mash the reserved coral and add it to the mayonnaise. Serve the mayonnaise separately.

Baked salmon

12 servings

1 (6–7 pound) whole salmon
4 tablespoons butter, melted
1 teaspoon salt
Freshly ground black pepper
2 tablespoons lemon juice
½ cup white wine
½ cup water

Cut a piece of aluminum foil large enough to envelop the salmon. Brush the foil generously with butter. Brush salmon on both sides with remaining butter. Sprinkle fish with salt, pepper and lemon juice. Wrap the salmon in foil and place in a roasting tin, or on a baking sheet. Bake in a 350° oven allowing 10 minutes per pound and 10 minutes extra. Pour combined wine and water over the fish after 20 minutes; this will prevent fish from drying out. Remove the fish from the oven. (The salmon will stay hot for several minutes if it remains wrapped in foil.) If it is served cold, keep the fish wrapped in foil to retain its shape.

Kippers are generally served for breakfast accompanied with freshly-made toast or brown bread and butter.

Grilled kippers

4 servings

4 kippers
4 tablespoons butter
4 teaspoons lemon juice
Fresh parsley for garnish

Remove kippers from packages and discard oil. Place kippers on a grillpan lined with aluminum foil. Dot each fish with butter and sprinkle with lemon juice. Grill fish 5 minutes on each side until skin is crisp and golden brown. Serve garnished with sprigs of parsley.

Herrings fried in oatmeal

4 servings

4 fresh herrings, cleaned or 1½ pounds salt water fish
½ cup milk
8 tablespoons oatmeal
1 teaspoon salt
Freshly ground black pepper
3 tablespoons butter or margarine

Mustard sauce:
2 tablespoons butter
2 tablespoons flour
1¼ cups milk
2 teaspoons prepared (Dijon type) mustard
1 teaspoon lemon juice

Dry the fish on paper towels. Dip fish first in milk and then in oatmeal. Season fish with salt and pepper. Heat the butter in a large skillet. Fry herrings 5 minutes on each side, adjusting the heat to prevent the butter from burning. Serve with mustard sauce prepared as follows: Heat 2 tablespoons butter in a small saucepan. Stir in the flour and cook 1 minute. Add milk gradually stirring constantly to form a smooth sauce. Add mustard and lemon juice. Season with salt and pepper. Serve sauce separately.

Grilled mackerel with gooseberry sauce

Grilled mackerel with gooseberry sauce

4 servings

1½ pounds mackerel, cleaned and washed
¼ cup olive oil
2 tablespoons lemon juice
1 small onion, finely chopped
4 tablespoons finely chopped parsley
½ teaspoon salt
Freshly ground black pepper

Gooseberry sauce:
1 pound canned gooseberries or cranberries, drained
Reserved syrup from gooseberries, plus water to measure 1 cup
2 tablespoons butter
1 tablespoon flour
1 tablespoon chopped parsley
½ teaspoon tarragon or fennel

In a bowl, combine the oil, lemon juice, onion, parsley, salt and pepper. Dry the fish on paper towels and make 4 or 5 diagonal cuts in the skin on each side, using a sharp knife. Place the fish in a shallow baking dish. Pour oil mixture over the fish and let it stand 1 hour. Turn the fish every 15 minutes. Drain fish and grill 8 minutes on each side.
In the meantime prepare the sauce: Place the gooseberries with 1 cup reserved syrup and water in a blender and blend until smooth. Strain the purée to remove gooseberry skins and seeds. Melt the butter in a small saucepan. Stir in the flour and cook 1 minute.
Add gooseberry purée. Stir in parsley and tarragon or fennel. Serve the sauce separately.

Salmon Kedgeree

Salmon with rice

3 servings

1 cup cooked rice
1 (12 ounce) can salmon, drained
1 large tomato, peeled, seeded and chopped
½ cup heavy cream, whipped
½ teaspoon salt
Dash tabasco sauce
1 tablespoon lemon juice
⅓ cup grated Parmesan cheese
1 tablespoon butter

In a bowl, combine rice, salmon, tomato, cream, salt, tabasco and lemon juice. Place mixture in a small buttered baking dish. Sprinkle with cheese and dot with butter. Bake uncovered in a 400° oven for 8 to 10 minutes until salmon is hot and cheese is bubbling.
Note: Ham dipped in a batter and deep fried is sometimes served with this dish. To prepare a batter for the ham, see recipe on page 28.

THE TIMES
Printing House Square, London, EC4P 4DE Telephone: 01-236 2000
THE PERNICIOUS DANGER
COOPER'S
FORD"

Fish cakes

4 servings

1 pound cod
1 tablespoon butter
½ teaspoon salt
Freshly ground black pepper
1 teaspoon lemon juice
4 medium sized potatoes, boiled and peeled
¼ cup milk
½ cup all purpose flour
2 eggs, lightly beaten
½ cup breadcrumbs
Oil for deep frying

Place the fish in a buttered baking dish. Dot with remaining butter. Season with salt, pepper and lemon juice. Cover dish with a piece of aluminum foil. Bake 20 minutes in a 350° oven. Remove skin and bones from the fish and flake into small pieces. Force potatoes through a strainer or potato ricer. Add potatoes to fish. Add enough milk to allow mixture to hold together. Form mixture into 8 flat patties. Dredge patties with flour, dip quickly into egg and finally into breadcrumbs. Fry fish cakes for 4 to 5 minutes in deep hot fat until golden brown on both sides.

Potted shrimp

4 servings

½ cup butter
¾ pound very small shrimp, peeled
¼ teaspoon salt
Dash cayenne pepper
¼ teaspoon ground mace
¼ teaspoon nutmeg
¼ teaspoon allspice

Heat the butter in a small saucepan. When butter is hot and foaming, remove from the heat and strain through a double thickness of cheesecloth to remove deposits. Reserve 2 tablespoons clarified butter. Heat remaining butter in a small skillet. Add shrimp seasonings and spices. Cook over high heat for 5 minutes, taking care to prevent the butter from burning. Place in a small pot and chill in the refrigerator. Pour on reserved clarified butter to seal the pot. Serve as a cocktail spread on freshly made toast or crackers.

Shrimp with mustard and eggs

6 servings

2 pounds small shrimp, peeled and deveined
4 scallions, finely chopped
3 tablespoons butter
2 tablespoons finely chopped parsley
½ teaspoon tarragon
1 tablespoon mild (Dijon type) mustard
6 hard boiled eggs, finely chopped
¼ cup heavy cream
3 tablespoons grated Parmesan cheese
1 additional teaspoon butter

Melt the butter and sauté the shrimp and scallions over high heat for 3 minutes until shrimp are pink and almost tender. Reserve 6 partially cooked shrimp. Add the parsley, tarragon, mustard, eggs and cream. Continue cooking for 2 minutes until the eggs are hot. Transfer all the ingredients to a buttered baking dish. Sprinkle with cheese, dot with remaining butter and add reserved shrimp. Place under the grill for 3 minutes until lightly browned.

Crab salad

4 servings

1¼ pounds fresh backfin crabmeat
1 tablespoon lemon juice
1 cup mayonnaise
½ cup sour cream
1 teaspoon Worcestershire sauce
3 tablespoons prepared shrimp cocktail sauce
2 ripe tomatoes, sliced
1 small cucumber, sliced
3 hard boiled eggs, sliced
⅓ cup English walnuts, chopped
1 avocado, sliced

Clean the crab carefully to remove hard membranes. Sprinkle crabmeat with lemon juice. Combine mayonnaise, sour cream, Worcestershire sauce and shrimp cocktail sauce. Allow the sauce to stand for 1 hour if possible. Arrange the tomato, cucumber and egg slices around the edges of 4 plates. Place the crabmeat in the center of the circle. Top crab with walnuts. Arrange avocado around the crabmeat.

Mussels or clams in broth

4 servings

- 2 *quarts fresh mussels or clams or 2 (1 pound) cans mussels or clams*
- 1 *cup dry white wine*
- 1 *cup water*
- ½ *teaspoon salt*
- 4 *scallions, finely chopped*
- ½ *teaspoon dried thyme*
- 2 *bay leaves*
- 4 *tablespoons finely chopped parsley*
- 1 *stalk celery, very finely chopped*
- 1 *tablespoon butter, softened*
- 1 *tablespoon flour*

Scrub the mussels with a stiff brush and clean well. Remove beards. Place mussels in a large bowl and cover with cold water. Discard any open mussels. Soak mussels 15 minutes to allow sand to soak out. Rinse mussels and place in a saucepan. Add wine and water. Add salt, scallions, thyme, bay leaves, parsley and celery. Cover and simmer 5 minutes. Strain liquid from the pan into a small saucepan and return to simmer. Combine butter and flour into a paste. Stir paste into simmering broth. Remove top shells from each mussel. Place in individual soup bowls and cover with the sauce.

Oysters

4 servings

- 24 *fresh oysters*
- 1 *lemon, cut into wedges*
- *Tabasco sauce or cayenne pepper*
- 4 *slices brown bread*
- *Butter*

Insert the oyster knife close to the hinge in the shell. Twist the knife upwards across the hinge to open the oyster. Slip the knife under the oyster to release it from the shell. (This will also kill the oyster.)
Place the shells on serving plates filled with crushed ice. Garnish the plates with lemon wedges. Serve tabasco sauce or cayenne pepper separately. Serve the oysters immediately accompanied with buttered brown bread.

Baked trout and bacon

2 servings

- 2 *(¾ pound) trout, filleted*
- 8 *slices bacon*
- 2 *tablespoons butter*
- 2 *tablespoons chopped parsley*
- ½ *teaspoon salt*
- *Freshly ground black pepper*

Dry trout thoroughly on paper towels. Line a baking dish with half of the bacon. Place half of the butter and parsley in each trout cavity and season with salt and pepper. Lay trout on the bacon and cover with remaining bacon. Bake in 350° oven for 15 minutes. Discard bacon and serve trout with boiled potatoes.

Baked trout and bacon, recipe page 27, 4th column

Fried fish and chips

4 servings

1½ pound fish, e.g. halibut, cod or flounder
1 tablespoon lemon juice
½ cup flour

Batter:
1 cup flour
1 teaspoon salt
Freshly ground black pepper
1 teaspoon paprika
1 cup beer or milk

Chips:
3 large baking potatoes
1 teaspoon coarse salt
Oil or shortening for deep frying

Cut the fish into medium sized pieces allowing 2 pieces for each serving. Sprinkle the fish with lemon juice. Combine the ingredients for the batter in a bowl stirring with a wire whisk until smooth. Peel the potatoes. Cut into slices and then into strips. Place the strips (chips) in a bowl of iced water for 5 minutes. Drain potatoes and dry them on paper towels. Heat the fat to 375°. Fry the potatoes until they are almost tender, but not browned. Drain chips on paper towels. Dredge the fish in flour and then dip in the batter. Fry the fish for 5 minutes in the same fat in which chips were cooked. Remove the fish from the fat. Increase the heat under the fat until it regains a temperature of 375°. Lower the fish into the hot fat and continue cooking for 3 or 4 minutes until batter is crisp and golden and the fish is done. Drain the fish and keep it warm in a 300° oven. Return the chips to the fat and fry for 3 or 4 minutes until tender, crisp, and golden. Drain the chips and sprinkle with coarse salt. Serve the fish and chips immediately, wrapping them first in wax paper and then in today's newspaper! **Note:** The batter for the fish is not the traditional, slightly soggy, British batter, but is delicate, light and crisp. We recommend the use of beer rather than milk; though milk may be used in an emergency. It is also possible to serve the fish and chips on a plate, but they tend to lose something in translation! In the fish and chip shops, vinegar is always available for seasoning the fish and chips.

Fried fish and chips, recipe page 28, 4th column

Shrimp with mustard and eggs, recipe page 26, 3rd column

Meat dishes

Scenes from the world-famous twelfth-century tapestry about the Battle of Hastings between William the Conqueror and the English, showing the slaughtering of the cattle, the roasting of the meat, the laying of the table and the feast that followed.

Boiled beef with horseradish

8 servings

- 4 *pounds fresh or salt brisket or corned beef*
- 4 *onions, sliced*
- 4 *carrots, sliced*
- 3 *stalks celery, sliced*
- 2 *bay leaves*
- 3 *sprigs parsley*
- 1 *teaspoon thyme*
- 1 *teaspoon black peppercorns*
- 3 *cups water*

Sauce:

- ½ *cup heavy cream, whipped*
- ½ *cup sour cream*
- 4 *teaspoons prepared horseradish*
- ½ *teaspoon salt*

Place the beef in a heavy casserole. Add the remaining ingredients. Add enough water to cover the beef. This quantity will vary, depending on the size of the casserole. Add 1 teaspoon salt if fresh beef was used. Cover casserole and simmer for 3 hours until the meat is tender when pierced with a fork. Chill the meat in the strained broth overnight. Remove the fat which will have risen to the surface of the broth. Slice the beef thinly. Reheat the sliced beef in the broth until it is just hot. Do not overcook the beef. Combine the ingredients for the sauce. Arrange slices of meat on a serving plate. Serve a variety of boiled vegetables separately. Serve the sauce separately.

Shropshire herb roll

4 servings

Pastry:

- 2 *cups sifted all purpose flour*
- 1 *teaspoon salt*
- ½ *pound beef suet, chilled and chopped into small pieces*
- 1 *tablespoon lemon juice*
- 6 *tablespoons water*

Filling:

- 2 *tablespoons finely chopped parsley*
- ¼ *teaspoon thyme*
- 1 *tablespoon finely chopped chives*
- ½ *teaspoon marjoram*
- ½ *teaspoon chervil*
- 1 *onion, finely chopped*
- 1 *egg, lightly beaten*
- ½ *pound bacon, fried until crisp*
- 2 *cups leftover chicken, cut into small pieces*
- 2 *tablespoons milk*

Sauce:

- 1 *tablespoon butter*
- 1 *tablespoon flour*
- ½ *cup beef broth*
- 1 *tablespoon Madeira*

Place the flour and salt in a bowl. Add the suet and blend the suet into the flour with a pastry blender or fingertips. Add the lemon juice. Stir the water into the flour with a fork, adding just enough water to form the pastry into a ball. Wrap the ball in waxed paper and chill it for 1 hour. Dust the pastry with flour and roll it into a rectangle about 12 inches by 8 inches in size. Combine the herbs, onion and egg and spread onto the pastry. Add crumbled bacon and chicken. Season with salt and pepper. To prepare the sauce, melt the butter and add the flour. Stir in the beef broth gradually to form a thick sauce. Add the Madeira. Pour sauce over the bacon and chicken and roll the pastry lengthwise as for a Swiss roll. Pinch the ends together to contain the filling. Place the roll on a buttered and floured cookie sheet. Brush the roll with milk and bake in a 400° oven for 15 minutes. Reduce the heat to 350° and continue cooking for 30 minutes or until golden brown.

Baked ham

10 servings

- 5–6 *pound smoked tenderized ham*
- 2 *cups orange juice*
- 4 *cloves*
- 1 *(2 pound) can apricots*
- ½ *cup apricot preserves*
- 2 *tablespoons sherry*
- 2 *tablespoons mild (Dijon type) mustard*
- 1 *cup brown sugar*

Place the ham in a roasting pan, fat side up. Add orange juice and cloves. Add syrup from canned apricots. Roast uncovered in a 350° oven allowing 30 minutes to the pound. One hour before the estimated cooking time has elapsed, take the ham from the oven. Remove the rind and leave a layer of fat about ¼ inch thick. Draw criss cross lines in the fat. Heat and then strain the apricot preserves. Add sherry and mustard. Brush ham with mixture and then press sugar over the ham. Return the ham to the oven to complete the cooking. Serve the ham hot or cold with a garnish of apricot halves.

Stewed oxtail

4 servings

- 1 *(2½ pound) oxtail, cut into joints*
- ½ *cup flour seasoned with*
  1 teaspoon salt
  Freshly ground black pepper
- 3 *tablespoons vegetable oil*
- 2 *onions, finely chopped*
- 2 *carrots, sliced*
- 1 *small turnip, diced (optional)*
- 2 *stalks celery, chopped*
- 2 *cups beef broth*
- 1 *bay leaf*
- ½ *teaspoon thyme*
- 1 *tablespoon lemon juice*
- 1 *tablespoon tomato paste*
- 2 *tablespoons finely chopped parsley*

Dredge the oxtail joints in seasoned flour and then brown the joints in hot oil. Transfer the joints to a casserole. Fry the onions, carrots, turnip and celery in the same oil. Stir in 1 tablespoon seasoned flour. Add the beef broth and all the remaining ingredients except the parsley. Cover and cook in a 300° oven for 3 hours until the meat is tender. Chill the stew overnight. Remove the fat which has risen to the surface. Reheat the casserole in a 350° oven for 20 minutes. Garnish with parsley and serve with boiled potatoes.

Pot roast beef

6 servings

- 3 *pounds boneless chuck steak, cut in 1 piece and tied*
- 2 *tablespoons oil*
- 3 *onions, chopped*
- 3 *carrots, chopped*
- 1½ *cups beef broth*
- 1 *tablespoon tomato paste*
- 1 *bay leaf*
- 3 *sprigs parsley*
- ½ *teaspoon thyme*
  Freshly ground black pepper
- 1 *teaspoon salt*
- 1½ *tablespoons butter, softened*
- 1½ *tablespoons flour*

Brown the beef on all sides in very hot oil. Remove the beef. Add onions and carrots to the same oil and cook for 5 minutes. Place beef and vegetables in a casserole. Add broth, tomato paste, bay leaf, parsley, thyme, pepper and salt. Cover and cook in a 350° oven for 2½ hours until beef is tender. Discard bay leaf and parsley. Combine butter and flour in a custard cup, blending until smooth. Stir into liquid in the casserole. Cook 4 minutes until liquid is thickened into a sauce. Slice the beef, spoon the sauce over the beef and serve with boiled potatoes and freshly cooked vegetables.

North country beef

3 servings

- *$1\frac{1}{2}$ pounds flank steak*
- *1 onion, finely chopped*
- *1 tablespoon finely chopped parsley*
- *$\frac{1}{2}$ cup red wine*
- *1 tablespoon Worcestershire sauce*
- *$\frac{1}{2}$ cup beef broth*
- *1 tablespoon cornflour dissolved in 2 tablespoons cold water*

Draw criss cross lines across the steak with a sharp knife. Combine the onion and parsley and press the mixture into the scored beef. Place the beef in a shallow dish. Add the wine and Worcestershire sauce. Allow the beef to marinate in the wine for 1 hour, or longer if possible. Turn the beef once. Remove the beef from the marinade. Dry on paper towels. Grill the beef 4 minutes on each side.
In the meantime, place the wine and Worcestershire sauce in a small saucepan. Add the beef broth and bring to boiling point. Stir in the cornflour dissolved in cold water and allow the mixture to thicken into a sauce.
Slice the beef thinly, holding the knife almost flat and parallel to the beef. Cut long thin slices of beef, cutting across the grain. Serve the sauce on the beef.

Roast beef

6 servings

- *6 pound best rib*

Sauce:

- *2 tablespoons fat from roast*
- *3 scallions, finely chopped*
- *2 tablespoons flour*
- *$\frac{1}{2}$ cup beef broth*
- *$\frac{1}{2}$ cup red wine*
- *$\frac{1}{4}$ teaspoon thyme*
- *$\frac{1}{4}$ teaspoon salt*
- *Freshly ground black pepper*

Stand beef, fat side up, in a roasting pan. Insert a meat thermometer taking care that the thermometer does not touch the bone. Roast the beef uncovered in a 450° oven for 15 minutes. Lower the heat to 350°. Allow 18 minutes to the pound for rare beef (thermometer reading 130°), 25 minutes (150°) for medium rare beef and 30 minutes for well done beef (165° on the thermometer). Remove the beef from the oven and wrap in aluminum foil. Allow the beef to stand for 15 minutes before carving. While the beef is reassembling all its juices, prepare the sauce.
Place 2 tablespoons of fat from the roast in a small saucepan. Sauté scallions in the fat 3 minutes. Stir in the flour and allow the flour to brown in the fat for 1 minute. Add beef broth, wine and thyme. Season with salt and pepper. Simmer sauce uncovered for 10 minutes.

Roast beef

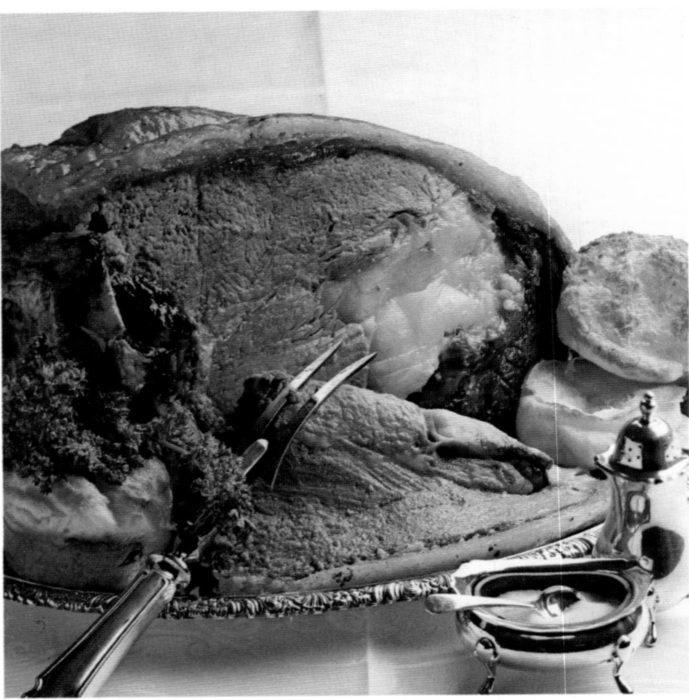

North country beef

Bacon and eggs are the pillar of the classic English breakfast, and one of the most attractive features of breakfast for continental visitors who are used to croissants and coffee.

British bacon and eggs

4 servings

16 slices thick bacon
8 eggs
4 slices bread, cut into halves
2 tablespoons butter
1 tablespoon oil

Fry the bacon in its own fat until crisp. Drain bacon and transfer to a warm plate. Fry eggs in the bacon fat, spooning a little of the fat over the eggs to set the whites firmly. In the meantime, fry the bread on both sides in hot combined butter and oil until bread is crisp and golden. Drain bread on paper towels. Serve bacon and eggs on hot plates. Arrange fried bread on the plate.

Pork chops with orange

8 servings

- 8 *pork chops*
- ½ *cup flour seasoned with 1 teaspoon salt Freshly ground black pepper and 1 teaspoon dry English mustard powder*
- 2 *eggs, lightly beaten*
- 1 *cup breadcrumbs*
- 2 *tablespoons butter*
- 1 *tablespoon oil*
- 2 *oranges, peeled and sliced*
- 2 *tablespoons finely chopped parsley*

Dredge the chops in seasoned flour. Dip into egg and then coat with breadcrumbs. Brown the chops on both sides in hot combined butter and oil. Continue cooking 8 minutes on each side until meat is tender. In the meantime, place sliced oranges on a plate. Cover with another plate and place over a pan of simmering water over low heat. Steam oranges 5 minutes until they are hot. Arrange the crisp pork chops on a bed of rice. Garnish with parsley and orange slices.

Meat loaf

6 to 8 servings

- 2 *tablespoons butter*
- 2 *medium sized onions, finely chopped*
- 3 *stalks celery, finely chopped*
- 1 *clove garlic, crushed*
- 1½ *pounds ground beef*
- ½ *cup breadcrumbs*
- 1 *teaspoon sage, thyme or marjoram*
- 2 *tablespoons finely chopped parsley*
- 1 *egg, lightly beaten*
- 1 *tablespoon tomato paste*
- ¼ *cup red wine or beef broth*
- 6 *slices bacon*

Heat the butter and sauté onions and celery until softened. Add garlic. Combine these ingredients with all of the remaining ingredients except the bacon. Place in a buttered round mold. Cover with bacon strips. Bake in a 350° oven for 1½ hours. Discard the bacon and pour off the accumulated fat. Invert onto a serving plate. Serve with mashed potatoes.

Faggots

Baked liver rolls

6 servings

- 1½ *pounds calves' liver, ground by the butcher*
- 1 *to 1½ cups breadcrumbs*
- 2 *tablespoons butter*
- 2 *onions, finely chopped*
- 1 *egg, lightly beaten*
- 1 *teaspoon sage*
- 2 *tablespoons finely chopped parsley*
- ½ *teaspoon salt Freshly ground black pepper*

Combine ground calves' liver with breadcrumbs. Heat the butter in a small skillet and fry the onions 3 minutes until softened. Add the butter and onions to the liver mixture. Remove from the heat. Stir in the egg, sage, parsley, salt and pepper. Form the mixture into 12 balls. Place balls in a buttered baking dish. Cover the dish with foil and bake in a 350° oven for 40 minutes.

Stuffed sirloin steak

4 servings

- 2 *(1 pound) boneless sirloin steaks*
- 1 *tablespoon butter*
- 1 *tablespoon vegetable oil*
- 1 *small onion, finely chopped*
- 8 *medium sized mushrooms, finely chopped*
- 2 *slices boiled ham, diced*
- 1 *teaspoon lemon juice*
- 2 *tablespoons finely chopped parsley*
- 1 *teaspoon thyme*
- 1 *teaspoon salt Freshly ground black pepper*
- 4 *tablespoons breadcrumbs*

Cut the steak horizontally, cutting the meat almost in half to form a deep pocket to contain the filling. Heat the butter and oil and fry the onion for 3 minutes. Add mushrooms and cook for another 3 minutes. Remove from the heat and stir in all the remaining ingredients. Sandwich the filling into the steaks and secure with a poultry lacer or tie with string. Brush steaks with oil. Grill the steaks 6 minutes on each side.

Roast loin of pork

6 servings

- $2\frac{1}{2}$ *pounds boneless pork loin, cut in 1 piece*
- 1 *teaspoon salt*
- *Freshly ground black pepper*
- 1 *teaspoon dried rosemary*
- 2 *tablespoons finely chopped parsley*

Tie the pork at 3 inch intervals to retain the shape during the cooking process. Cut criss cross lines in the fat with a sharp knife. Season pork with salt and pepper. Chop rosemary and parsley together and press into the scored fat. Place pork on a rack in a roasting pan. Roast pork uncovered in a 350° oven for $1\frac{3}{4}$ hours. Serve hot with applesauce or baked apples.

Lamb chops and tomato sauce

4 servings

- 8 *loin lamb chops*
- $\frac{1}{2}$ *cup flour*
- 2 *eggs, beaten*
- 1 *cup breadcrumbs*
- 4 *tablespoons parsley*
- *Grated rind of 1 lemon*
- 1 *teaspoon salt*
- *Freshly ground black pepper*
- 4 *tablespoons butter*
- 1 *tablespoon oil*
- $1\frac{1}{2}$ *pounds spinach, cooked*
- 8 *slices lemon*
- 1 *cup prepared tomato sauce*

Dredge lamb chops in flour and dip into beaten egg. Combine breadcrumbs, parsley, lemon rind, salt and pepper. Coat lamb chops with breadcrumb mixture. Heat 2 tablespoons of butter in a large skillet. Add oil. Fry lamb chops in combined hot butter and oil allowing 10 minutes on each side. Purée the spinach in a blender adding remaining 2 tablespoons of butter. Place hot spinach on a serving plate. Arrange lamb chops on the spinach. Garnish with lemon slices and serve tomato sauce separately.

The stew must be among the oldest dishes known to mankind. The same man who discovered how to make the first rude pot out of wet clay probably went on to put together vegetables and meat to stew over a wood fire. And over the thousands of years since, each of the world's nations has had ample time to develop its own distinctive stew. If anyone doubts that you can tell a nation and its people by their stew, just ask him whether there can be anything more Irish in the world than Irish stew. The flavor of a good Irish stew – the combination of mutton, cabbage, onions and potatoes – is unique. It is the flavor of Ireland: the picturesque cottages in the undulating hills of this, the greenest of all islands. The secret of a good stew is patience. The distinct flavors of the different ingredients, the meat, vegetables, potatoes, and herbs, must come together slowly, they must blend gradually so that they can all be tasted separately, but still form a perfect combination. In small Irish cottages, stews were simmered in massive iron pots over slow, smouldering peat fires until they reached flavor perfection. If you prepare Irish stew remember to keep the fire as low as possible so that it will have the same effect as the slow burning peat. Only then will the juices of the mutton, the onions, the potatoes, and the full flavor of the cabbage all blend evenly together.

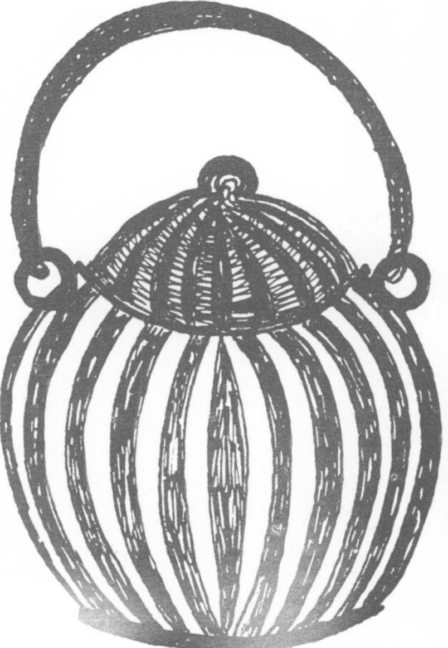

A real Irish lamb stew should actually be cooked in an iron kettle hanging from a chain over an open peat fire, (but a lamb stew out of the oven tastes just as good)!

Irish lamb stew

6 servings

- *3 pounds stewing lamb*
- *6 large all purpose potatoes*
- *4 yellow onions*
- *2 tablespoons finely chopped parsley*
- *1 teaspoon thyme*
- *1 teaspoon salt*
- *Freshly ground black pepper*
- *1½ cups chicken broth*
- *1½ tablespoons butter, softened*
- *1 tablespoon flour*
- *2 tablespoons finely chopped parsley for garnish*

Cut the lamb into slices or cubes. Peel the potatoes and onions and cut them into thin slices or chunks.
Chop the parsley and thyme together. Butter a casserole. Arrange a layer of ⅓ of the potatoes on the bottom of the casserole. Cover with a layer of lamb, then a layer of onions. Season with the herbs, salt and pepper. Repeat to form 3 layers, seasoning between each layer and ending with the onions. Add the broth. Cover the casserole and cook in a 350° oven for 1½ hours until the lamb is tender. Combine the butter and flour in a custard cup and add the paste into the casserole. Continue cooking 5 minutes until the juices are thickened. Garnish with parsley.

Beef olives

Roast rack of lamb, recipe page 38, 3rd column

Beef olives

6 servings

1½ pounds top side of beef cut into 6 slices measuring approximately 5 inches by 3 inches
½ pound sausage meat
1 onion, finely chopped
3 tablespoons breadcrumbs
Grated rind of 1 lemon
1 teaspoon salt
Freshly ground black pepper
1 egg, lightly beaten
2 tablespoons oil
1½ cups beef broth
1 teaspoon tomato paste
1 tablespoon butter, softened
1½ tablespoons flour
2 tablespoons parsley, finely chopped

Ask the butcher to flatten and tenderize beef slices with a cleaver. To prepare the filling for the beef: cook the sausage until the fat has rendered. Discard the fat and place sausage meat in a bowl. Add onion, breadcrumbs, lemon rind, salt and pepper. Stir in egg to bind the mixture together. Spread part of the filling on each piece of beef. Roll and tie the beef. Brown the beef lightly in hot oil and then place in a baking dish. Add broth and tomato paste. Cover with foil and cook in a 350° oven for 1½ hours. Combine butter and flour and stir into beef broth. Simmer 5 minutes until liquid has thickened into sauce. Garnish with parsley.

Haricot mutton

Lamb stew with beans

4 servings

1½ pounds stewing lamb without bones
2 tablespoons oil
2 small onions, chopped
2 cloves garlic, crushed
1 carrot, diced
2 tablespoons flour
1½ cups beef broth
1 bay leaf
3 sprigs parsley
½ teaspoon thyme
½ teaspoon salt
Freshly ground black pepper
1 cup dried lima beans

Trim the lamb and cut into cubes. Brown lamb in hot oil and transfer to a casserole. Fry onions, garlic and carrot in the same oil for 3 minutes. Stir in the flour and cook 1 minute. Add broth, bay leaf, parsley, thyme, salt and pepper. Cover the casserole and cook in a 350° oven for 1½ hours until lamb is tender. Remove bay leaf and parsley sprigs. In the meantime, wash the beans. Place beans in a saucepan and add 4 cups cold water. Bring water to boiling point. Simmer beans for 5 minutes. Turn off the heat and allow beans to soak for 1 hour. Drain beans and discard soaking water. Bring 4 cups water to simmering point. Add 1 teaspoon salt and the beans. Cover and simmer 1½ hours until beans are tender. Drain beans and add to lamb in the casserole.

Note: 2 cups cooked canned beans or frozen beans may be used to replace dried beans in this recipe. Like all stews, this dish is best prepared a day in advance and reheated in a 350° oven for 20 minutes.

Roast rack of lamb

4 servings

4 pound rack of lamb (8 chops cut into 1 piece)
1 tablespoon coarse salt
Freshly ground black pepper
2 tablespoons finely chopped parsley
2 cloves garlic, crushed
¼ teaspoon thyme
¼ teaspoon tarragon
1 tablespoon finely chopped fresh chives
¾ cup freshly made breadcrumbs
2 tablespoons butter, melted

Ask the butcher to strip the fat from the bones and trim the cut edges of the bone to a length of 3 inches from the outer edge of the meat. Score the fat covering the meat with a sharp knife. Sprinkle the meat with salt and pepper. Combine the herbs and garlic. Press half of the herb mixture into the meat. Place on a rack in a roasting pan. Roast lamb uncovered in a 400° oven for 30 minutes. Remove fat from the lamb. Combine remaining herb mixture with breadcrumbs. Press mixture onto the lamb. Drizzle with melted butter. Return the lamb to the oven and continue cooking for 15 minutes until lamb is tender and the breadcrumbs are lightly browned. Garnish with watercress and tomatoes stuffed with cooked peas. Serve with mashed potato croquettes.

Crown roast of lamb

8 servings

1 whole loin (16 ribs) Spring lamb, prepared by the butcher for a crown roast
4 tablespoons butter
2 small onions, finely chopped
1 clove garlic, crushed
2 stalks celery, chopped
½ pound sausage meat
2½ cups fresh breadcrumbs
3 tablespoons chopped parsley
2 tablespoons chopped chives
½ teaspoon thyme
½ teaspoon rosemary
½ teaspoon salt
Freshly ground black pepper
¼ cup white wine or chicken broth

Place the lamb in a roasting tin and brush meat all over with 2 tablespoons melted butter. Wrap pieces of foil around cut bone ends to prevent them from burning. Prepare the herb filling: Heat remaining 2 tablespoons of butter and cook onions, garlic and celery for 5 minutes until softened. Cook sausage separately until fat has rendered. Combine cooked sausage with onion mixture and remove from the heat. Stir in breadcrumbs, parsley, chives, thyme, rosemary, salt and pepper. Moisten mixture with wine or broth. Fill into the center of the roast. Cover filling with aluminum foil to prevent it from drying out. Roast lamb in a 350° oven for 3 hours. Remove foil and decorate cut bone ends with chop frills. Add freshly cooked peas to cover herb filling in the center of the crown.

Stuffed shoulder of lamb

6 servings

- *1 (4 pound) shoulder of lamb, boned*
- *½ pound sausage meat*
- *2 tablespoons butter*
- *1 onion, finely chopped*
- *1 stalk celery, finely chopped*
- *2 tablespoons finely chopped parsley*
- *1 teaspoon mint*
- *1 teaspoon salt*
- *Freshly ground black pepper*
- *1 egg, lightly beaten*
- *2 tablespoons vegetable oil*
- *1 tablespoon lemon juice*

Fry the sausage meat in a skillet over low heat for 8 minutes until the fat has rendered. Discard the fat and place partially cooked sausage meat in a bowl. Heat the butter and fry the onion and celery 3 minutes until softened. Combine with sausage meat and stir in remaining ingredients except oil and lemon juice. Spread this mixture over the inner surface of the lamb. Roll the lamb tightly and tie it with string at 2 inch intervals. Place the lamb on a rack in a roasting pan. Brush with combined oil and lemon juice. Roast uncovered in a 375° oven for 1½ hours. Baste the lamb frequently.

Toad in the hole

Sausage in batter

4 servings

- *1 pound small pork sausages*
- *1 cup milk*
- *2 eggs*
- *1 cup all purpose flour*
- *½ teaspoon salt*
- *Freshly ground black pepper*
- *1 tablespoon butter, melted*

Fry the sausage until lightly browned and all the fat has rendered. Place sausages in a 9 inch square baking dish. To prepare the batter, place milk, eggs, flour, salt, pepper and butter in a blender. Blend 1 minute until smooth. Pour batter over the sausages and bake uncovered in a 400° oven for 30 minutes. The batter will become puffed, crisp and golden brown.

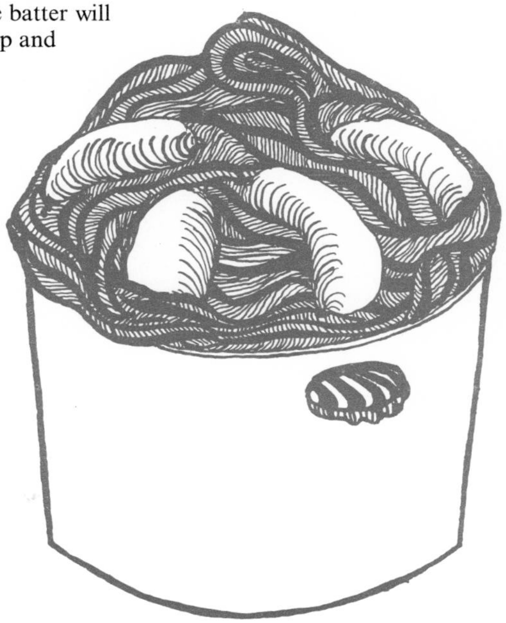

Sausage and mash

4 servings

- *8 pork sausages*
- *6 medium sized potatoes, mashed*
- *¼ cup milk*
- *2 tablespoons butter*
- *¼ cup Parmesan cheese, grated*
- *⅛ teaspoon nutmeg*
- *½ teaspoon salt*
- *Freshly ground black pepper*
- *1 medium sized onion, sliced and separated into rings*
- *Oil for deep frying*

Fry the sausages in a skillet until lightly browned and all the fat has rendered. Mash the potatoes adding the milk, 1 tablespoon of butter, cheese, nutmeg, salt and pepper. Place a layer of half of the potatoes in a buttered baking dish. Arrange the sausages over the potatoes. Place remaining potatoes in a pastry bag fitted with a large rosette tube. Pipe potatoes in a decorative pattern around the sausages. Dot with remaining butter and bake in a 400° oven for 10 minutes. In the meantime, deep fry the onion rings in hot oil for 5 minutes until tender and lightly browned. Drain onions on paper towels. Garnish dish with onion rings and serve very hot.

Oysters and lamb are a strange combination: but in Lancashire, they have both and so why not put them in the same pot? The result is suprisingly good.

Lancashire hot pot

6 servings

- *2 tablespoons butter*
- *6 baking potatoes, peeled and sliced ¼ inch thick*
- *2 pounds stewing lamb, cut into slices 1 inch thick*
- *1 teaspoon salt*
- *Freshly ground black pepper*
- *2 onions, sliced thinly*
- *3 lambs kidneys, cut into small pieces*
- *12 oysters*
- *1 cup beef broth*
- *2 tablespoons finely chopped parsley*

Butter a 1½ quart casserole. Place a layer of ¾ of the potato slices in the dish and cover with the lamb. Season with salt and pepper. Cover with a layer of ½ of the onion slices. Add the kidneys, then a layer of remaining onions. Add the oysters and top with a layer of potatoes. Add the beef broth. Brush potatoes with melted butter. Cover and cook in a 350° oven for 2 hours. Remove the lid and return the dish to the oven for 30 minutes to allow the potatoes to become crisp and brown.

Poultry and game dishes

Roast turkey with stuffing,
recipe page 42, 1st column

Roast turkey with stuffing

12 servings

1 (10 pound) turkey
2 tablespoons butter or margarine, softened
1 teaspoon salt
Freshly ground black pepper
1 teaspoon paprika

Dressing:
2 pounds sausage meat
2 tablespoons butter
2 medium sized onions finely chopped
2 stalks celery, finely chopped
1 cup English walnuts, chopped
Liver from turkey, chopped
4 tablespoons finely chopped parsley
1 teaspoon salt
Freshly ground black pepper
2 cups breadcrumbs, freshly made
3 eggs, lightly beaten

Giblet gravy:
Giblets from turkey
2 onions, finely chopped
2 stalks celery, stems and leaves
1 bay leaf
3 sprigs parsley
½ teaspoon salt
1 teaspoon peppercorns
1 cup white wine
1½ cups chicken broth
3 tablespoons butter
3 tablespoons flour

To prepare the dressing: Fry sausage meat until all the fat has rendered. Place sausage meat in a bowl. Heat the butter and fry the onions, celery, nuts and turkey liver for 5 minutes over moderate heat. Add these ingredients to the sausage. Stir in all the remaining ingredients and fill into the turkey cavity. Secure dressing with poultry skewers.
Rub the outside skin of the turkey with softened butter. Season with salt, pepper and paprika. Place the turkey on a rack in a roasting pan.
Roast uncovered in a 325° oven for 3½ hours. (Allow 15 minutes additional time for each extra pound of turkey.)
Place giblets, onions, celery, bay leaf, parsley, salt, pepper, wine and broth in a saucepan. Cover and simmer over very low heat for 1½ hours. Strain the broth. When the turkey has cooked, skim the fat from the juices in the roasting pan. Pour the liquid into the broth. Add butter to the roasting tin. Place tin over low heat and allow the butter to melt.
Stir in the flour. Add ½ cup cold chicken broth and scrape up the brown pieces clinging to the bottom of the pan. Add reserved strained chicken broth. Stir to form a medium thick gravy.

Roast chicken

4 servings

1 (3½ pound) roasting chicken
2 tablespoons butter, softened
1 teaspoon salt
Freshly ground black pepper

Sage and onion dressing:
3 onions, coarsely chopped
1 cup breadcrumbs, freshly made
1 tablespoon sage
½ teaspoon salt
Freshly ground black pepper
2 tablespoons butter, melted

Bread sauce:
2 cups milk
2 onions, finely chopped
2 cloves
½ teaspoon salt
Dash cayenne pepper
1 bay leaf
1½ cups breadcrumbs, freshly made

To prepare the dressing: cook the onions in boiling, salted water for 15 minutes until softened. Drain the onions. Place in a bowl and stir in remaining ingredients. Fill dressing into the chicken cavity and secure with poultry skewers. Rub chicken with butter and season with salt and pepper. Place chicken on a rack in a baking dish. Roast uncovered in a 350° oven for 1 hour and 15 minutes.
To prepare the bread sauce: bring the milk to simmering point in a saucepan. Add onions, cloves, salt, pepper and bay leaf. Simmer 15 minutes and strain the milk. Stir in breadcrumbs and serve the sauce hot.

Chicken breasts with lemon and brandy

6 servings

6 whole chicken breasts (12 single breasts), with skin and bones removed
½ cup flour seasoned with salt and pepper
1 teaspoon oregano
3 tablespoons butter
2 tablespoons lemon juice
2 tablespoons brandy, warmed
2 tablespoons finely chopped parsley

Combine the flour, salt, pepper and oregano. Dredge the chicken breasts in the seasoned flour. Fry breasts in hot butter 6 minutes on each side until white and tender. Do not overcook. Add lemon juice and brandy. Light the brandy with a match. When the flames have died down, serve the chicken breasts on a bed of boiled rice. Spoon the pan juices over the chicken and garnish with chopped parsley.

Chicken with oysters

4 servings

- 4 *whole chicken breasts (8 separate chicken breasts)*
- ½ *teaspoon salt*
- *Freshly ground black pepper*
- *Juice of ½ lemon*
- 4 *fresh oysters*
- 1½ *cups chicken broth*
- ½ *cup dry white wine*

Sauce:

- 2 *tablespoons butter*
- 2 *tablespoons flour*
- 1 *egg yolk*
- ¼ *teaspoon salt*
- *Freshly ground black pepper*
- 1 *teaspoon lemon juice*
- 2 *tablespoons finely chopped parsley*

Split each breast in half. Sprinkle breasts with salt, pepper and lemon juice. Place an oyster in the center of 4 breasts. Cover with the remaining 4 halves. Wrap each serving tightly in aluminum foil. Place the packets in a flameproof casserole just large enough to hold them. Pour on the broth and wine and bring to a simmer. Cover and cook slowly for 20 minutes. Remove the packets and keep warm. Reduce the cooking liquid over high heat to 1½ cups. In a saucepan, melt the butter and add the flour. Cook, stirring, 1 minute. Add the reduced cooking liquid gradually, beating with a wire whisk until a thick sauce has formed. Remove from the heat and beat in the egg yolk. Season with salt, pepper and lemon juice. Remove the chicken breasts from the foil and arrange on a serving platter. Top with the sauce and garnish with parsley.

Note: Do not reheat the sauce after the egg yolk has been added or it will curdle.

Welsh chicken

6 servings

- 1 *(4 pound) chicken*
- ½ *pound bacon*
- 2 *large leeks or 6 scallions, diced*
- 3 *carrots, diced*
- 3 *tablespoons flour*
- 1 *small cabbage, shredded*
- ¼ *teaspoon dried thyme*
- ¼ *teaspoon dried marjoram*
- ¼ *teaspoon dried chervil*
- 1 *tablespoon finely chopped parsley*
- ½ *teaspoon salt*
- *Freshly ground black pepper*
- 2 *cups chicken broth*
- 1 *tablespoon melted butter*

Wash the chicken, dry it thoroughly inside and out and truss it. In a heavy flameproof casserole, cook the bacon until crisp. Remove it from the pan, crumble and set aside. Discard all but 2 tablespoons of bacon fat. In the reserved fat, sauté the leeks and carrots until soft. Stir in the flour and cook 1 minute. Add the reserved bacon, cabbage, herbs, salt, pepper and broth and bring to a simmer. Place the chicken in the casserole and pour on the melted butter. Cover the chicken with foil, then a lid and simmer slowly 2 hours or until chicken is tender. Remove chicken from casserole. With a slotted spoon, transfer the cabbage to a serving dish. Remove trussing strings from chicken and place on the bed of cabbage. Coat the chicken with a little of the sauce and pass the rest separately.

Farmhouse chicken casserole

6 servings

- *2 (2½ pound) chickens, cut into serving pieces*
- *1 cup flour seasoned with 1 teaspoon salt and Freshly ground black pepper*
- *2 tablespoons butter*
- *1 tablespoon oil*
- *12 small white onions*
- *12 small new potatoes, peeled*
- *8 mushrooms, cut into quarters*
- *6 slices bacon, fried until crisp and crumbled*
- *2 cups chicken broth*
- *1 tablespoon cornflour dissolved in 2 tablespoons cold water*
- *2 tablespoons finely chopped parsley*

Dredge chicken pieces in seasoned flour. Heat the butter and oil in a large skillet and fry the chicken until golden brown. Transfer the chicken to a casserole. Add onions and potatoes to the skillet and cook until lightly browned. Shake the skillet occasionally to prevent potatoes from sticking. Transfer onions and potatoes to the casserole. Add mushrooms to the skillet and cook over moderately high heat for 4 minutes. Place mushrooms in the casserole. Add crumbled bacon and chicken broth. Cover the casserole and place in a 350° oven for 50 minutes. Thicken juices with cornflour dissolved in cold water. Garnish with parsley.

Creamed chicken

6 servings

- *1 (5 pound) chicken*
- *1 medium sized onion, spiked with 6 cloves*
- *3 stalks celery, cut in 1 inch pieces*
- *2 carrots, cut in 1 inch pieces*
- *1 medium sized turnip, quartered*
- *½ teaspoon mace or nutmeg*
- *1 teaspoon salt Freshly ground black pepper*
- *2 tablespoons butter*
- *4 tablespoons flour*
- *½ cup cream Juice of 1 lemon*
- *2 tablespoons finely chopped parsley*

Place the chicken, onion, celery, carrots, turnip, mace, salt and pepper in a heavy casserole. Add water to cover and bring to a boil over high heat. Reduce the heat, cover and simmer slowly 1½ hours or until chicken is tender. Remove the chicken. Strain the broth and chill it 4 hours until the fat rises to the top. Discard the chicken skin and bones and slice the meat. Remove the fat from the broth. In a saucepan, melt the butter. Stir in the flour and cook 1 minute. Add 2 cups of the broth and stir vigorously with a wire whisk until the sauce has thickened. Stir in the cream and lemon juice. Add the sliced chicken and heat through. Serve the creamed chicken on freshly made toast, in vol au vent cases or over rice. Garnish with parsley.

Chicken with mushrooms

2 servings

- *1 (2 pound) chicken, cut into serving pieces*
- *2 tablespoons butter*
- *1 tablespoon vegetable oil*
- *½ teaspoon salt Freshly ground black pepper*
- *1 tablespoon lemon juice*
- *1 onion, finely chopped*
- *4 mushrooms, finely chopped*
- *4 slices bacon, fried until crisp*
- *1 cup chicken broth*
- *1 tablespoon cornflour dissolved in 2 tablespoons cold water*

Brown the chicken pieces in hot combined butter and oil. Place the chicken in a small casserole and season with salt, pepper and lemon juice. Fry onion in the same butter and oil for 3 minutes. Add and cook mushrooms for 3 more minutes. Transfer these ingredients and the bacon, crumbled, to the casserole. Add the chicken broth. Cover and cook in a 350° oven for 50 minutes. Stir in cornflour paste and simmer over direct heat for 2 minutes until sauce has thickened.

Chicken with vegetables

4 servings

- *1 (3½ pound) chicken*
- *½ teaspoon salt Freshly ground black pepper*
- *1 teaspoon tarragon*
- *2 tablespoons butter*
- *1 tablespoon vegetable oil*
- *2 onions, finely chopped*
- *2 carrots, diced*
- *2 stalks celery, diced*
- *1¼ cups chicken broth*
- *1 tablespoon cornflour dissolved in 2 tablespoons cold water*
- *2 tablespoons finely chopped parsley for garnish*

Season the cavity of the chicken with salt, pepper and ½ teaspoon tarragon. Heat the butter and oil in casserole and brown the chicken on all sides. Remove the chicken and add the vegetables. Cook 3 minutes and return the chicken to the casserole. Add the chicken broth and season the outside of the chicken with salt, pepper and remaining ½ teaspoon of tarragon. Cover the casserole and place in a 350° oven for 50 minutes. Cut the chicken into serving pieces. Combine the cornflour and water and stir the paste into the liquid over direct heat. Spoon the sauce over the chicken and garnish with parsley.

Roast duck with apple stuffing

4 servings

1 (4 pound) duck
1 tablespoon butter, softened

Dressing:
2 tablespoons butter
1 onion, finely chopped
3 stalks celery, finely chopped
1 green cooking apple, peeled, cored and sliced
¼ teaspoon cinnamon
½ teaspoon salt
Freshly ground black pepper
Rind of 1 lemon
1½ cups breadcrumbs, freshly made
½ cup apple cider

To prepare the dressing: melt 2 tablespoons butter in a skillet. Fry the onions, celery and apple 3 minutes until softened. Remove from the heat and stir in the remaining ingredients. Fill the dressing into the cavity of the duck and secure with poultry skewers. Prick the duck skin with a fork in several places to allow the fat to drain. Rub the duck skin with softened butter and season lightly with salt and pepper. Place the duck on a rack in a roasting tin. Roast uncovered in a 350° oven for 1½ hours until the duck is tender. Cut duck into quarters and serve hot or cold.

Chicken with tomatoes

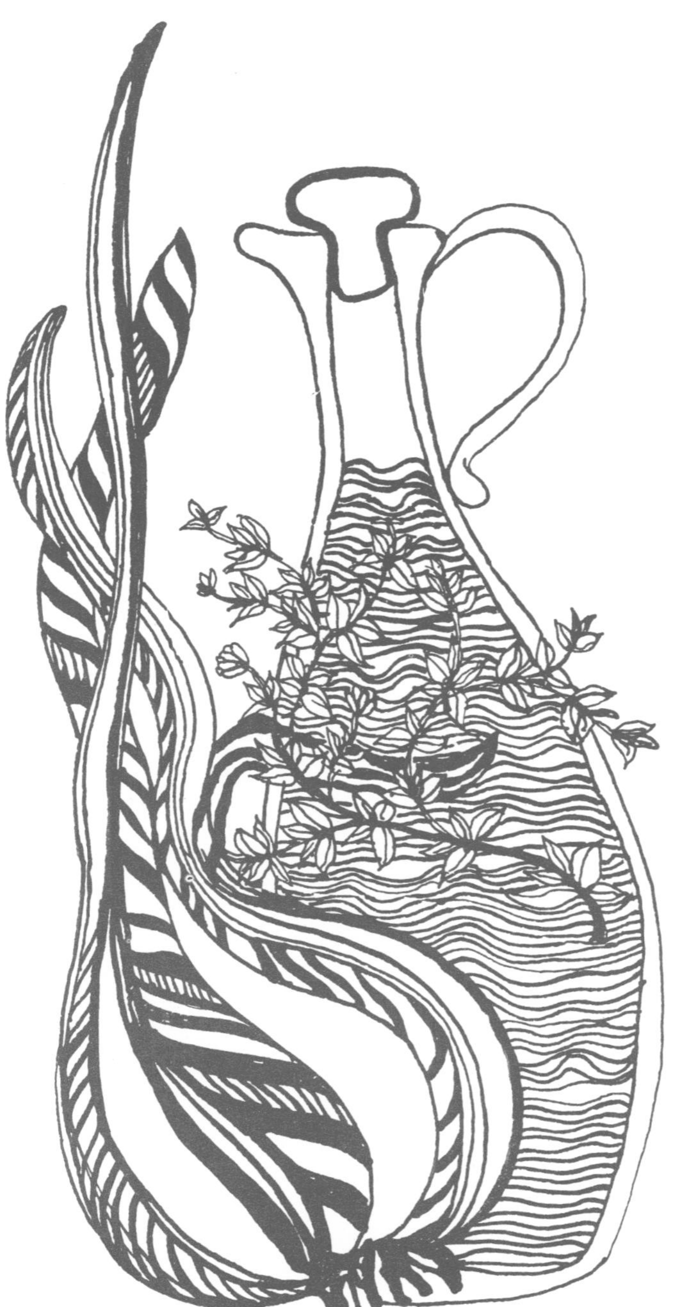

6 servings

2 (2 pound) chickens, cut into serving pieces
2 tablespoons butter
1 tablespoon oil
1 teaspoon salt
Freshly ground black pepper
2 medium sized onions, chopped
2 cloves garlic, crushed
3 medium sized tomatoes, peeled and seeded
1 teaspoon tomato paste
½ teaspoon basil
1½ cups chicken broth
1 tablespoon cornflour dissolved in
2 tablespoons cold water
2 tablespoons finely chopped parsley
12 black pitted olives

Brown the chicken pieces in hot combined butter and oil. Remove the chicken and season with salt and pepper. Cook the onions and garlic in the same oil for 3 minutes. Add 2 of the tomatoes, cut into thin wedges. Add tomato paste, basil and chicken broth.
Replace the chickens. Cover the casserole and cook in a 350° oven for 50 minutes. Arrange the chicken pieces on a bed of rice. Strain the pan juices and return to a clean saucepan. Stir in cornflour dissolved in cold water. Add remaining tomato, cut into wedges, and heat 3 minutes until sauce is hot. Spoon the sauce over the chicken and garnish the plate with parsley and black olives.

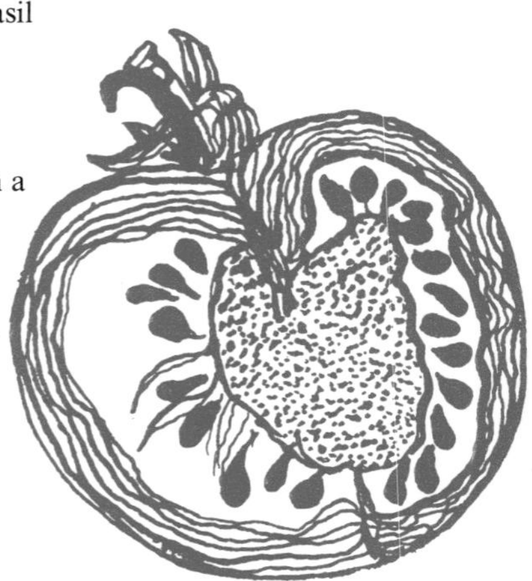

West country chicken

6 servings

- *2 (2½ pound) chickens, cut into serving pieces*
- *2 tablespoons butter*
- *1 tablespoon vegetable oil*
- *2 onions, finely chopped*
- *1 clove garlic, crushed*
- *6 mushrooms, thinly sliced*
- *2 tablespoons flour*
- *1½ cups chicken broth*
- *½ teaspoon salt*
- *Freshly ground black pepper*
- *6 slices bacon, fried until crisp*
- *2 tomatoes, peeled, seeded and chopped*
- *2 tablespoons finely chopped parsley*

Brown the chicken in combined hot butter and oil. Transfer the chicken pieces to a casserole. Fry the onions and garlic in the same fat for 3 minutes. Add and fry the mushrooms for 3 minutes. Lower the heat and stir in the flour. Add the chicken broth gradually, stirring to form a medium sauce. Season with salt and freshly ground black pepper. Transfer all these ingredients to the casserole. Drain and crumble the bacon. Add bacon and tomatoes to the casserole. Cover and cook in a 350° oven for 50 minutes. Garnish with parsley. Serve on a bed of rice.

Baked chicken

4 servings

- *2 (2 pound) frying chickens, cut into serving pieces*
- *1 cup breadcrumbs, freshly made*
- *1 teaspoon salt*
- *Freshly ground black pepper*
- *1 teaspoon rosemary*
- *2 tablespoons finely chopped parsley*
- *2 tablespoons butter*

Combine breadcrumbs, salt, pepper, rosemary and parsley. Roll the chicken pieces in seasoned breadcrumbs. Place in a buttered baking dish. Dot the chicken with butter and bake uncovered in a 350° oven for 1 hour. Serve with grilled tomato halves and fried or boiled potatoes.

Chicken patties

4 servings

- *2 cups left over cooked chicken*
- *4 scallions, finely chopped*
- *3 slices boiled ham, diced*
- *2 hard boiled eggs, finely chopped*
- *1 tablespoon lemon juice*
- *1 teaspoon mild (Dijon type) mustard*
- *4 tablespoons butter*
- *4 tablespoons flour*
- *1 cup milk*
- *½ teaspoon tarragon*
- *1 tablespoon finely chopped chives*
- *½ cup flour, seasoned with*
- *1 teaspoon salt*
- *Freshly ground black pepper*
- *2 eggs, lightly beaten*
- *½ cup breadcrumbs*
- *Oil or shortening for deep frying*

Shred the chicken into very small pieces. Place in a bowl and combine with scallions, ham, eggs, lemon juice and mustard. Heat the butter in a small saucepan. Stir in the flour and add the milk gradually, stirring with a wire whisk to form a very thick "sauce". Add tarragon and chives. Stir the sauce into the chicken mixture. Chill the mixture in the refrigerator for 2 hours. Form chicken into 8 patties. Dredge patties first in flour, then in beaten egg and finally in the breadcrumbs. Fry the patties in deep hot fat for 8 to 10 minutes until hot and lightly browned.

Cumberland chicken

6 servings

- *2 (2½ pound) chickens, cut into serving pieces*
- *2 tablespoons butter*
- *1 tablespoon oil*
- *6 slices bacon, fried until crisp*
- *2 onions, finely chopped*
- *1 clove garlic, crushed*
- *4 mushrooms, quartered*
- *3 tablespoons flour*
- *2 cups chicken broth*
- *1 tablespoon tomato paste*
- *3 tomatoes, peeled, seeded and chopped*
- *½ teaspoon salt*
- *Freshly ground black pepper*
- *2 tablespoons finely chopped parsley*

Brown the chicken pieces in a skillet in combined hot butter and oil. Transfer chicken to a large casserole. Add drained and crumbled bacon to casserole. Fry onions and garlic in the same oil for 3 minutes until softened. Add mushrooms and cook 3 minutes. Stir in the flour and add 1 cup of the chicken broth gradually, stirring to form a thick sauce. Add tomato paste and tomatoes. Transfer all these ingredients to the casserole. Add remaining chicken broth and season with salt and pepper. Cover and cook in a 350° oven for 1 hour. Garnish with chopped parsley.

Pies and savoury puddings

Steak and kidney pie

Veal and ham pie

Steak and kidney pie

6 servings

- ½ *recipe for short crust pastry on page 65*
- 2 *pounds chuck steak, cubed*
- 4 *calves' kidneys*
- 3 *tablespoons oil*
- 3 *onions, finely chopped*
- 2 *tablespoons flour*
- 1½ *cups beef broth*
- ½ *teaspoon salt*
- *Freshly ground black pepper*
- 1 *tablespoon Worcestershire sauce*
- 1 *bay leaf*
- 1 *egg yolk*
- 1 *tablespoon milk*

Trim the beef to remove all the fat. Chop the kidneys into small pieces. Brown the beef and kidneys in hot oil. Add the onions and cook 5 minutes. Stir in the flour and add the beef broth gradually. Season with salt and pepper. Add Worcestershire sauce and bay leaf. Transfer all the ingredients to a casserole. Cover and simmer for 1½ hours until the beef is tender. Transfer ingredients to a deep 10 inch pie plate. Top steak and kidney with pastry. Cut a design deeply into the pastry to allow the steam to escape. Brush pastry with egg yolk and milk glaze. Bake in a 350° oven for 35 minutes until beef is hot and pastry is golden brown.

Veal and ham pie

4 servings

- ½ *teaspoon marjoram*
- 2 *tablespoons finely chopped parsley*
- *Grated rind of 1 lemon*
- ½ *teaspoon salt*
- *Freshly ground black pepper*
- 1 *tablespoon flour*
- 1 *teaspoon butter*
- 1 *pound fillet of veal (veal scallopini) cut into thin strips*
- 4 *slices boiled ham, cut into 2 inch strips*
- 1 *hard boiled egg, sliced*
- ¾ *cup beef broth*
- 4 *frozen prepared puff pastry shells, defrosted*
- 1 *egg yolk*
- 1 *teaspoon heavy cream or milk*

In a bowl, combine the marjoram, parsley, lemon rind, salt, pepper and flour. Toss veal strips in the seasoning. Butter a 9″ pie dish and add a layer of ½ of the veal. Top with half of the ham and add all the egg slices. Repeat veal and ham layers. Add beef broth. Open a package of prepared puff pastry shells and knead 4 of the shells until softened. Roll pastry on a lightly floured board. Brush pastry with egg yolk combined with cream. Make a small hole in the center of the pastry to allow the steam to escape. Bake in a 350° oven for 1 hour. Serve hot or cold.

Yorkshire pudding

4 servings

- 1 *cup milk*
- 2 *eggs*
- 1 *cup all purpose flour*
- 1 *teaspoon salt*
- 3 *tablespoons rendered hot fat from roast beef or 3 tablespoons hot oil or butter*

Place the milk, eggs, flour, salt and 2 tablespoons hot fat in a blender and blend until smooth. Pour 1 tablespoon fat into a 9 inch pie plate. Pour in the batter. Bake in a 425° oven for 15 minutes. Reduce the heat to 350° and continue cooking for another 15 minutes until the pudding is puffed and a crisp brown. Cut into wedges and serve immediately with roast beef.

Shepherd's pie

6 servings

- 2 *pounds ground beef*
- 1 *tablespoon oil*
- 2 *onions, finely chopped*
- 2 *carrots, finely chopped*
- 1 *tablespoon tomato paste*
- 1 *tablespoon flour*
- 1 *cup beef broth*
- 1 *cup cooked mixed vegetables, either frozen vegetables or a combination of left over vegetables*
- 5 *medium sized potatoes, boiled and mashed*
- 1 *tablespoon butter*

Brown the beef in oil and discard the accumulated fat. Stir in the onions and carrots and continue cooking for 5 minutes. Stir in the tomato paste, flour and broth. Add the cooked vegetables. Transfer all the ingredients to a casserole or deep 9 inch pie plate. Top with mashed potatoes, dot with butter and bake uncovered in a 350° oven for 30 minutes.

Since the days when Geoffrey Chaucer wrote in his 'Canterbury Tales' of 'hot pyes', the English have been making them in a thousand different varieties. Surely some day soon the thousand and first will be created. The English eat pies both at and away from home. The easiest and best-loved way to have a quick lunch in London is to pop into a pub and order a large piece of meat pie and a 'pint'. In any old English cookbook there are innumerable recipes for pies: with meat, with fish, with poultry, with fruit and vegetables, or with a mixture of all these. In the 15th and 16th centuries, when plates were still scarce and only the rich could afford knives and forks, the pie had an enormous advantage: the crust was both the plate and platter at the same time and there was no problem about using fingers to eat with.
Everything was, and is, put into the pies and even until well into the 19th century ingredients were as imaginative as they were plentiful. An old recipe from Staffordshire explains that in order to make a good pie, the cook should first take a cooked veal tongue, stuff it into a chicken, stuff the chicken into a large duck, and the duck into a turkey and finally stuff the turkey into a goose.
The goose was then placed on a dough crust and covered by another layer of dough. All the room that was left over inside the pastry shell was filled with

Cornish pie

ground meat and small birds. The pie was then popped into the oven. Naturally all the bones had been very carefully removed from the chicken, the duck, the turkey and the goose. It was certainly a recipe calling for an experienced kitchen maid to help!

The favorite dessert of Queen Elizabeth I was apple pie. So strongly was the apple pie the symbol for all that was desirable and pleasant that the 16th century poet Robert Green in one of his famous verses wrote: 'Thy breathe is like the steame of apple pies'. And the physician Cogan wrote in his medical book 'Haven of health' in 1612: 'They that will not eate apples may yet eate apple pies, which may be very wholesome for cholericke stomackes, if they be well made'.

6 servings

- *1 pound leg of lamb, cut into 1 inch cubes*
- *1 tablespoon butter*
- *1 cup beef broth*
- *2 onions, finely chopped*
- *2 medium sized raw potatoes, peeled and diced*
- *½ teaspoon salt*
- *Freshly ground black pepper*
- *½ recipe for pastry see page 65*
- *1 tablespoon cornflour dissolved in 2 tablespoons cold water*
- *1 egg yolk*
- *1 tablespoon heavy cream or milk*

Place the lamb in a heavy saucepan. Add butter, broth and onions. Place over moderate heat. Cover and simmer for 30 minutes. Add potatoes and cook another 10 minutes. Season with salt and pepper. Roll the pastry on a lightly floured board. Cut the pastry into 6 six inch circles. Drain meat mixture and place a little of the mixture in the center of each circle. Add cornflour paste to meat broth and cook over moderate heat for 2 minutes until a thick sauce has formed. Place 2 tablespoons sauce on the meat mixture. Dampen the edges of the pastry with water. Fold each pastry circle in half and press the edges with a fork to seal securely. Brush pastry with egg yolk combined with cream or milk. Place on a buttered and floured baking sheet and bake in a 350° oven for 35 minutes.

Cottage pie

6 servings

2 pounds ground lamb
2 onions, finely chopped
2 cloves garlic, crushed
1 tablespoon butter
1 tablespoon vegetable oil
3 carrots, diced
2 small tomatoes, peeled, seeded and chopped
1 tablespoon tomato paste
1 tablespoon flour
1 cup beef broth
½ teaspoon rosemary
1 cup cooked green beans
½ teaspoon salt
Freshly ground black pepper
6 medium sized boiled potatoes, mashed
1 tablespoon butter

Cook ground lamb in a skillet until lightly browned. Discard accumulated fat. Fry the onions and garlic in hot butter for 3 minutes until softened. Add carrots and cook 3 more minutes. Add tomatoes, tomato paste and flour. Add beef broth and rosemary. Stir in beef and vegetables. Season with salt and pepper. Place in a deep 9 inch pie plate. Top with a layer of mashed potatoes. Dot potatoes with butter and bake uncovered in a 350° oven for 30 minutes. Serve from the pie dish.

Chicken and potato pie

4 servings

3 tablespoons butter
1 onion, finely chopped
4 tablespoons flour
1 teaspoon mild (Dijon type) mustard
1½ cups chicken broth
½ cup heavy cream
1 (2 pound) chicken, roasted
1 cup boiled ham, diced
1 (4 ounce) can button mushrooms, drained
1 cup green peas, cooked until tender
2 tablespoons finely chopped parsley
1 teaspoon rosemary
4 potatoes, cooked and mashed
1 tablespoon butter, melted

Heat the butter in a saucepan. Add the onion and cook for 3 minutes. Stir in the flour and mustard. Add the chicken broth and cream gradually. Stir to form a medium thick white sauce. Cut the chicken into small bite sized pieces. Add chicken, ham, mushrooms, peas, parsley and rosemary to the sauce. Transfer all these ingredients to a 9 inch pie plate. Fill potatoes into a pastry bag fitted with a large rosette tube and pipe mashed potatoes around the edge of the plate (or arrange an attractive border of mashed potatoes around a dish using a spoon). Brush potatoes with melted butter and place in a 375° oven for 15 minutes. Brown potatoes under the grill for 3 minutes.

Trout pie

4 servings

4 (¾ pound) trout, filleted
2 tablespoons butter
4 scallions, finely chopped
Juice 1 lemon
½ teaspoon salt
Freshly ground black pepper
½ cup white wine
½ cup heavy cream
1 tablespoon cornflour, dissolved in
2 tablespoons cold water
¼ cup chopped almonds
¼ cup breadcrumbs
2 tablespoons finely chopped parsley
1 tablespoon butter

Rinse the trout under cold, running water. Pat the fish dry on paper towels. Butter a baking dish and sprinkle with scallions. Lay trout on the scallions and sprinkle with lemon juice, salt and pepper. Add the wine. Place in a 350° oven for 8 minutes until fish are almost tender. Place dish on direct heat and add cream. Bring to simmering point and stir in cornflour paste. Combine almonds, breadcrumbs and parsley. Dot with butter and place under the grill for 3 minutes until crumbs have browned.

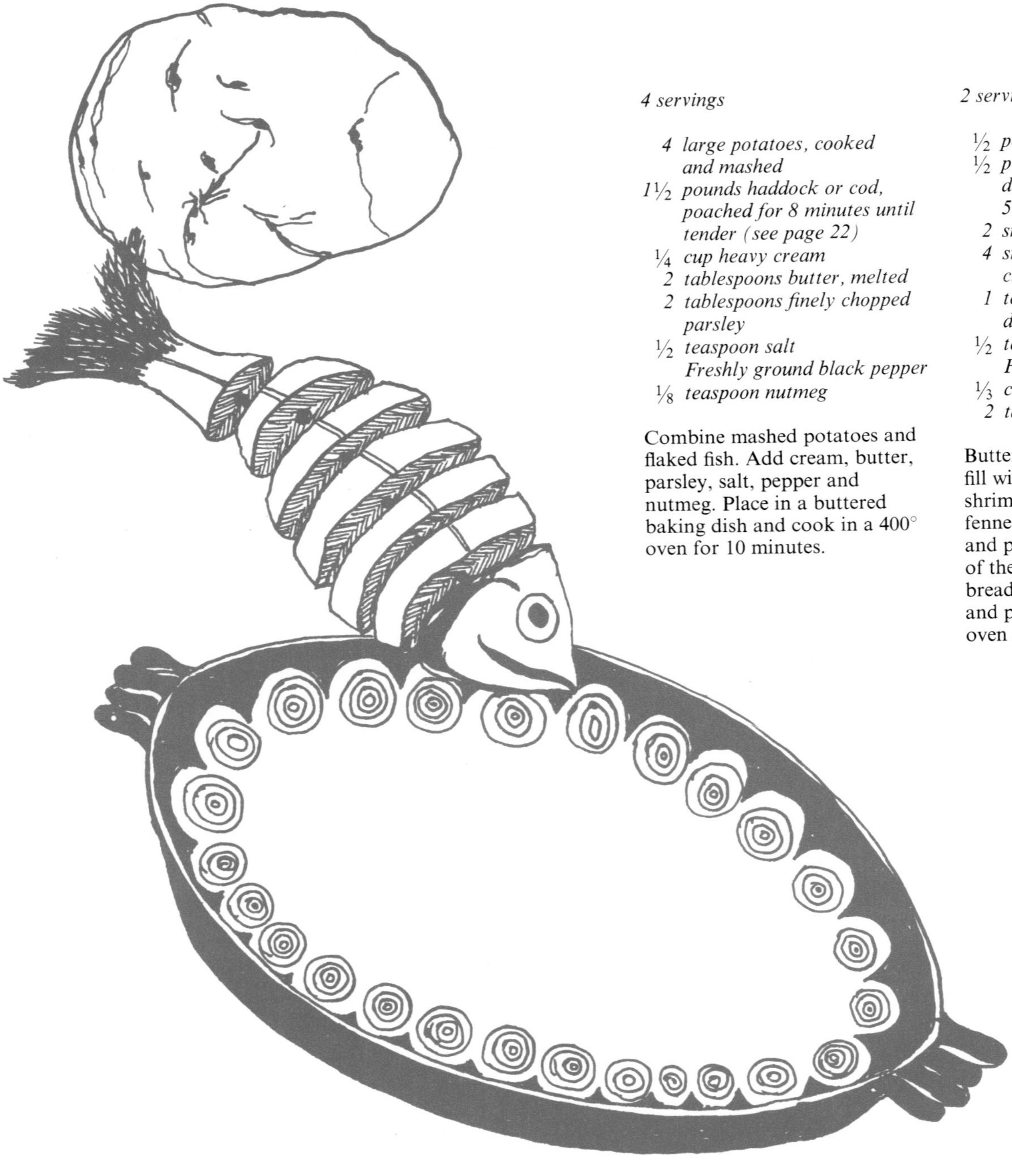

Haddock pie

4 servings

4 large potatoes, cooked and mashed
1½ pounds haddock or cod, poached for 8 minutes until tender (see page 22)
¼ cup heavy cream
2 tablespoons butter, melted
2 tablespoons finely chopped parsley
½ teaspoon salt
Freshly ground black pepper
⅛ teaspoon nutmeg

Combine mashed potatoes and flaked fish. Add cream, butter, parsley, salt, pepper and nutmeg. Place in a buttered baking dish and cook in a 400° oven for 10 minutes.

Halibut pie

2 servings

½ pound cooked halibut
½ pound small shrimp, peeled, deveined and boiled for 5 minutes
2 small ripe tomatoes
4 small scallions, finely chopped
1 teaspoon fennel weed or dill weed
½ teaspoon salt
Freshly ground black pepper
⅓ cup bread crumbs
2 tablespoons butter

Butter a small baking dish and fill with a layer of halibut, shrimp, tomato, scallion and fennel or dill. Season with salt and pepper. Add a second layer of these ingredients. Top with breadcrumbs. Dot with butter and place uncovered in a 400° oven for 10 minutes.

Shrimp pie

4 servings

2 tablespoons butter
2 tablespoons flour
1½ cups milk
1 teaspoon lemon juice
2 tablespoons shrimp cocktail sauce
2 tablespoons finely chopped parsley
½ teaspoon salt
Freshly ground pepper
½ pound macaroni, cooked
1 pound small shrimp, peeled, deveined and boiled 5 minutes
⅓ cup bread crumbs
1 tablespoon butter

Melt the butter in a saucepan. Stir in the flour and add the milk gradually, stirring with a wire whisk to form a smooth sauce. Stir in lemon juice, cocktail sauce, parsley, salt and pepper. Combine sauce with macaroni and shrimp. Place the mixture in a buttered baking dish. Top with breadcrumbs, dot with butter and place in a 400° oven for 10 minutes.

Fish mold

4 servings

1¼ pounds fresh salmon, cooked
2 cloves garlic, crushed
Juice ½ lemon
½ teaspoon salt
½ teaspoon dill weed
3 drops tabasco sauce
½ cup olive oil
½ cup heavy cream
½ cucumber, thinly sliced

Remove skin and bones from salmon. Place in a blender and add garlic, lemon juice, salt, dill weed and tabasco. Add oil. Turn on the motor and blend until smooth, adding the cream a few drops at a time. Blend until smooth. Pack mixture into an oiled bowl. Chill for 4 hours. Invert the bowl onto a serving dish and garnish mold with cucumber slices.

Vegetables and pickles

Potatoes in mustard sauce

4 servings

2 tablespoons butter
4 large potatoes
6 scallions, finely chopped
½ teaspoon salt
Freshly ground black pepper
⅛ teaspoon nutmeg
2 teaspoons prepared (Dijon type) mustard
2 teaspoons cornflour
1¼ cups milk, simmering

Butter a small baking dish. Peel potatoes and slice very thinly. Place a layer of ⅓ of the potatoes in the dish. Sprinkle with a few scallions and season with salt and pepper. Repeat to form 3 layers. Combine nutmeg, mustard, cornflour and ¼ cup hot milk in a small bowl. Add remaining milk and pour over the potatoes. Dot with butter. Cover the dish and bake in a 350° oven for 1 hour. Serve with roast meat or chicken or grilled fish.

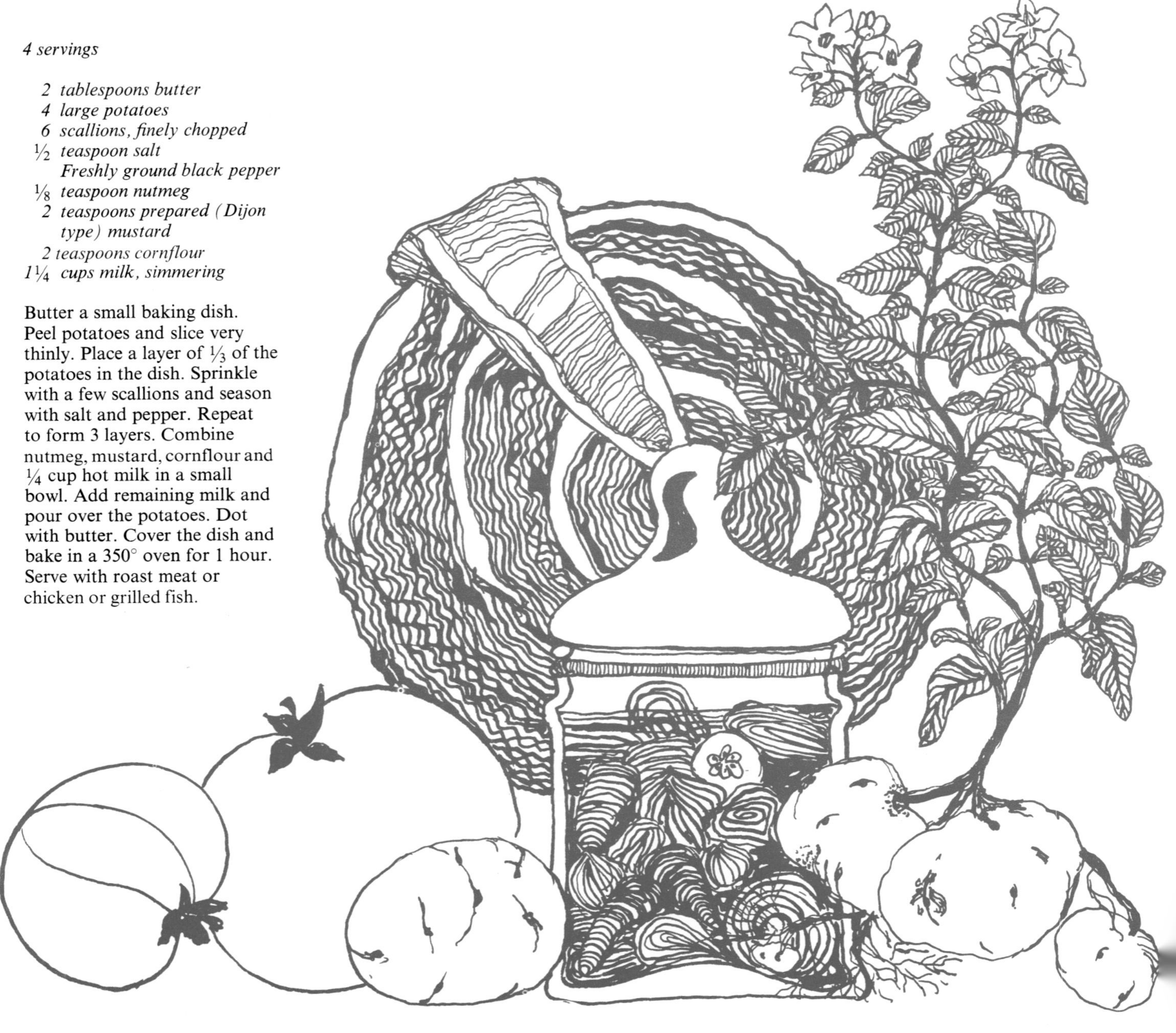

This may be a strange sounding dish to Americans, but it is dearly loved by the Irish. The bubbling and squeaking in the skillet as it cooks are the sounds of witches and ghosts trying to escape from the fiery heat! Not surprisingly, it is traditionally served on Halloween night.

Bubble and squeak

4 servings

- 3 *tablespoons butter or bacon fat*
- 1 *small onion, finely chopped*
- 2 *cups shredded cabbage, boiled for 15 minutes*
- 2 *cups mashed potatoes*

Heat the butter in a large skillet and fry the onion over low heat for 5 minutes until softened. Add cabbage and stir over low heat for 2 minutes. Fold in the mashed potatoes until well blended with the cabbage. Press mixture lightly onto the surface of the skillet to form a large pancake. Cook for 5 minutes until the underside has browned lightly. Turn and brown on the second side for five minutes.

Casserole of red cabbage

8 servings

- 2 *tablespoons butter*
- 1 *medium sized red cabbage, shredded*
- 1 *onion, finely chopped*
- 3 *medium sized cooking apples, peeled, cored and sliced*
- ¼ *cup red wine vinegar*
- ¼ *cup water*
- 2 *tablespoons brown sugar*
- 1 *teaspoon salt*
- *Freshly ground black pepper*

Butter a large casserole. Add the cabbage and all the remaining ingredients. Dot with butter. Cover casserole and cook in a 300° oven for 2½ hours. Serve with pork.

In England meat is simply roasted or braised and served without sauce. However, this leaves a longing for something just a little piquant. The English are famous for their pickles and piccalilli, which tastes specially good with cuts of cold meat.

Piccalilli

Mustard relish

Makes 6 (1 pint) jars

- *1 small cauliflower, divided into flowerets*
- *1 pound small white onions*
- *1 yellow onion, cut into small pieces*
- *1 cucumber, cut into small cubes*
- *2 underripe tomatoes, cut into small pieces*
- *2 cups green beans, cut into small pieces*
- *2 quarts cold water*
- *1 cup coarse salt*
- *6 tablespoons flour*
- *4 teaspoons English mustard powder*
- *2 teaspoons turmeric powder*
- *1 quart malt vinegar*
- *¼ cup sugar*

Combine all the cut vegetables in a large bowl. Dissolve the salt in the water and add to the vegetables. Cover and chill for 24 hours, turning the vegetables in the brine frequently. Drain the vegetables. To prepare the sauce, combine the flour, mustard and turmeric. Add ½ cup vinegar and stir to form a smooth paste. Transfer the paste to a large saucepan and add remaining vinegar gradually. Heat vinegar to boiling point. Add sugar and all of the vegetables. Simmer vegetables for 5 minutes in the sauce. Spoon into sterilized jars. The piccalilli may be served with cold meats after 24 hours.

Onions, cucumber and red cabbage are among the many vegetables which are used for pickling. The shelves in the cellar on which the pickles are stored are a great source of pride to many English housewives, recipe page 61, 4th column.

Pease pudding is a traditional English dish. Children in England skip rope to the old rhyme of:

'Pease pudding hot
Pease pudding cold
Pease pudding in the pot
Five days old...'

Cauliflower cheese

4 servings

1 medium sized cauliflower divided into flowerets
1 teaspoon salt
2 tablespoons butter
3 tablespoons flour
1½ cups milk
1 cup Cheddar cheese, grated
Dash cayenne pepper
4 tablespoons bread crumbs

Boil the cauliflower in salted water 10 minutes until almost tender. Drain cauliflower and place in a small buttered casserole. To prepare the sauce, melt the butter in a saucepan. Stir in the flour and add the milk gradually. Stir in ¾ cup grated cheese and cayenne pepper. Cook 2 minutes until the sauce has thickened. Pour the sauce over the cauliflower. Sprinkle with remaining cheese and breadcrumbs. Place in a 400° oven for 5 minutes and then under the grill for 3 minutes to brown the cheese and bread crumbs.

Pease pudding

Pea purée

6 servings

1 pound (2 cups) dried split green peas
3 cups water
1 teaspoon salt
1 teaspoon sugar
1 tablespoon lemon juice
3 tablespoons butter
Freshly ground black pepper

Wash peas thoroughly. Add salt to the water and bring water to boiling point. Add peas, sugar and lemon juice. Cover and simmer over low heat for 1½ hours until peas are tender. Drain the peas and force them through a sieve. Melt the butter in a skillet. Add peas and cook over low heat until the peas are hot, about 5 minutes. Season with freshly ground pepper and serve with boiled beef.

Apple chutney

Makes 3 (1 pint) jars

6 cups green cooking apples, peeled, cored and chopped
3 onions, roughly chopped
2½ cups seedless sultanas
2¼ cups brown sugar
2 cups cider vinegar
1 teaspoon salt
1 tablespoon mustard seeds, crushed
Dash cayenne pepper
2 red peppers, seeded and chopped (opt.)
1 tablespoon ginger root, grated or 1 teaspoon ground ginger
1 teaspoon pickling spice

Place all the ingredients in a large heavy pot. Simmer, uncovered, over low heat for 2½ hours until all the liquid has evaporated and the mixture has thickened. Stir occasionally to prevent sticking. Fill into sterilized jars and seal.

Pickles or relishes, have always commanded an important place on the English table. Some people believe that this is a result of England's age-old connections with India. Spices and curries from the East have certainly given new ideas and inspiration to England's cooking. But the English in fact have eaten pickles since time immemorial. Recipes can be found in old English cook-books as long ago as the 16th century. Then as now, pickles made with young, soft walnuts were special favorites. The English writer, Beverley Nichols, once found a manuscript inscribed in curious red ink and left in a forgotten closet of an old house. It contained a precious recipe for pickles with walnuts 'From Ye Lady Jepheris'. It read: 'Take your walnuts ye first full moon after midsummer, before they come to have any shell and boil them in severall waters to take away ye bitterness'. Then the nuts were shelled. It continues, 'Take their wait (weight) or somewhat more of good Loaf Shuger and put some water to it, then set it on ye fire and when it is scumd, put in the nuts to ye sirip, also 2 or 3 cloves and a nutmeg quartered'. The mixture was first simmered and then quickly boiled.

In another old recipe, this one from a collection in Sawson Hall Castle that dates back to the 17th century there are instructions for how 'to pickle wallnuts green, by that lovely, dear, charming, adorable, angelick creature, Miss Kitty Gibson'. It went on: 'Wrap them in Vine Leaves and then pour upon them hot Vinegar and let them lie a week. Then put them in fresh leaves and between every layer of nuts strew mustard, pepper, cloves, mace and horse-radish. Make the pickle of the best vinegar with a handfull of the same spice and pour it in them boiling hot. You may add garlick if you please. They are fit to eat in two months and will keep years'.

These must have been superb served with the roast beef that has been England's pride for centuries.

Pickled onions

Makes 2 (1 pint) jars

2 pounds small white onions
4 cups water
½ cup salt
1 quart malt vinegar
2 tablespoons pickling spices
4 cloves
2 bay leaves

Peel onions. Heat water and salt to boiling point. Pour salted water over the onions and leave onions to soak for 12 hours. Place vinegar, pickling spices, cloves and bay leaves in a saucepan. Cover and simmer for 10 minutes. Add onions and cook uncovered for 15 minutes. The onions should remain firm and crunchy. Transfer onions to to sterilized jars. Pour the vinegar over the onions. Cool and seal the jars. Allow the onions to marinate in the spiced vinegar for 1 month before serving. Serve as a sandwich accompaniment or with cold meats.

Pickled red cabbage

Makes 4 (1 pint) jars

2 small (3 pound) red cabbages
⅓ cup coarse salt
1 quart cider vinegar
3 cloves
¼ teaspoon nutmeg
2 bay leaves
2 tablespoons pickling spice
2 tablespoons sugar

Remove the core and heavy stems from the cabbage. Shred the cabbage into small pieces. Place cabbage in a large bowl. Stir in the salt and place in the refrigerator for 2 days. Stir cabbage 6 or 7 times to keep salt well distributed. Drain cabbage and squeeze it dry. Fill cabbage into jars. Pour vinegar into a saucepan and add the remaining ingredients. Boil uncovered for 5 minutes. Allow vinegar to cool. Strain vinegar and fill into jars. Seal the jars. Invert the jars once a day for 1 week before using. Use within 6 weeks. Serve with cold meats.

Boxty

Potato pancake

6 servings

- 4 *cups peeled and grated potatoes (about 2 pounds)*
- $1\frac{1}{3}$ *cups flour*
- 2 *teaspoons salt*
- 6 *tablespoons milk*
- 2 *tablespoons butter*
- $\frac{1}{4}$ *cup brown sugar*
- 4 *tablespoons melted butter*

Squeeze grated potatoes as dry as possible in a linen or terrycloth tea towel. In a bowl, combine the potatoes, flour and salt. Stir in the milk gradually, using just enough to make the mixture hold together. Let the mixture stand 1 hour. Heat a 9 to 10 inch heavy skillet until very hot. Drop in the butter and let it melt. Pat the potato mixture into the skillet with a spatula, distributing it evenly. Cook over medium heat until the underside is set and golden brown. Slide the pancake out onto a plate and invert it back into the skillet. Let the other side brown. Serve the pancake straight from the pan with brown sugar and melted butter.

Boxty is a traditional dish from Donegal, eaten on the eve of 'All Saints' Day.

Cauliflower cheese, recipe page 60, 1st column

Savouries

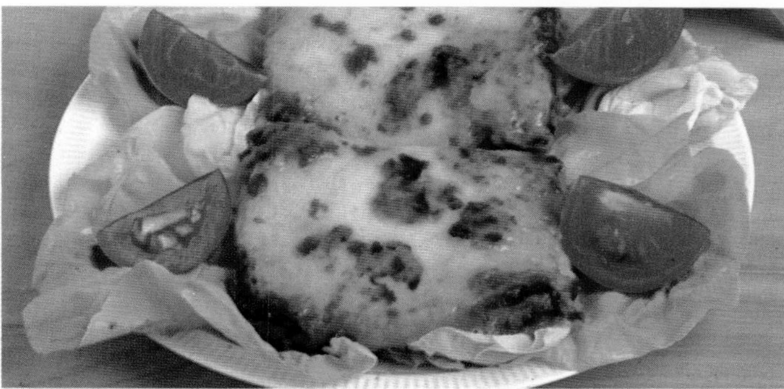

Scotch eggs

8 servings

- *1 pound sausage meat*
- *½ teaspoon sage*
- *2 tablespoons finely chopped parsley*
- *½ teaspoon thyme*
- *8 hard boiled eggs*
- *½ cup flour seasoned with*
- *½ teaspoon salt*
- *Freshly ground black pepper*
- *2 eggs, lightly beaten*
- *1 cup fine breadcrumbs*

Combine sausage meat, sage, parsley and thyme. Pat mixture into 8 rounds. Surround each hard boiled egg with a sausage pattie. Roll the eggs in the seasoned flour, then in the beaten eggs and finally in the breadcrumbs. Fry in deep hot fat 10 minutes until the sausage is cooked. Serve hot or cold.

Welsh rarebit (rabbit)

Cheese toasts

2 servings

- *1 cup Cheddar cheese (grated)*
- *3 tablespoons milk*
- *2 tablespoons butter*
- *¼ teaspoon salt*
- *Freshly ground black pepper*
- *1 teaspoon prepared (Dijon type) mustard*
- *2 slices toast, freshly made*

Place the cheese and milk in a saucepan. Stir over low heat until the cheese melts. Add butter, salt, pepper and mustard. Stir until butter melts. Spoon the mixture on the toast and brown under the grill for 2 minutes until lightly browned.

Note: Beer can be substituted for the milk in this recipe. The mixture may also be enriched with an egg yolk.

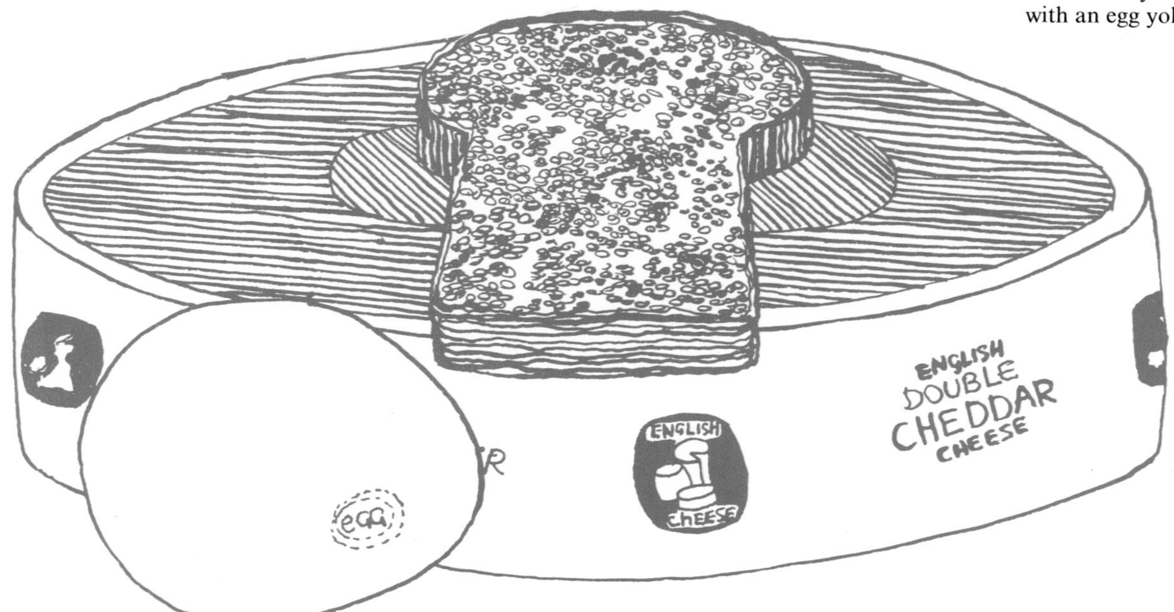

Devils on horseback

6 servings

- *12 large dried prunes or 12 black plums*
- *½ cup red wine*
- *1 bay leaf*

Stuffing:

- *a. 12 anchovy fillets, curled round 12 almonds*
- *b. 12 teaspoons chutney, chopped*
- *c. 12 pimiento stuffed olives*
- *6 thin slices bacon*
- *Watercress or parsley for garnish*

Place prunes or plums in a saucepan. Add wine and bay leaf. Simmer over low heat for 20 minutes until just tender. Cool prunes in the wine and remove pits. Fill each prune with one of the stuffings. Wrap ½ a bacon slice round each prune and secure with a toothpick. Place in a small baking dish. Heat in a 400° oven for 10 minutes until bacon is crisp. Drain on paper towels. Place on a serving dish and garnish with watercress or parsley.

Note: Devils on horseback may be served on small squares of hot buttered toast.

Angels on horseback

4 servings

- *8 fresh oysters*
- *4 thin slices bacon*
- *2 slices hot buttered toast, each cut into 4 squares*

Simmer the oysters in their own liquor over low heat for 4 minutes. Drain and wrap each oyster in half a slice of bacon. Secure bacon with tooth picks. Place under a hot grill or grill over charcoal until bacon is crisp. Serve on squares of hot buttered toast.

Sweet puddings – some like them hot

Rhubarb pie

8 servings

Short crust pastry:
2½ cups sifted all purpose flour
½ teaspoon salt
6 tablespoons butter, cut into small pieces
6 tablespoons margarine
6 tablespoons cold water

Filling:
4 cups rhubarb, cut diagonally into small pieces
1½ cups sugar
2 tablespoons butter, cut into small pieces
Grated rind of 1 orange
2 tablespoons cornflour dissolved in
¼ cup orange juice
½ teaspoon cinnamon
1 egg yolk
2 tablespoons milk
¼ cup icing sugar

Sift the flour into a bowl. Add the salt and the butter. Blend the butter into the flour using a pastry blender or fingertips. When the butter is the size of very small peas, blend in the margarine. Stir in the cold water with a fork adding 4 tablespoons first and then 1 tablespoon at a time. Add only enough water to form the dough into a ball. Wrap ball in wax paper and chill 20 minutes before using. Cut the pastry in half and roll on a lightly floured board. Fit the pastry into a 9 inch pie plate. Add rhubarb, sugar, butter and orange rind. Add cornflour paste and cinnamon. Cover with a second round of pastry. Brush top crust with egg yolk combined with milk. Bake in 375° oven for 30 minutes until crust is golden. Dust with sifted icing sugar
and serve warm or cold with sweetened whipped cream.

Pancakes

Crêpes

Makes 12–14 crepes

1¼ cups milk
1 egg
1 egg yolk
1 cup all purpose flour
¼ teaspoon salt
1 tablespoon butter, melted or 1 tablespoon oil
½ cup sugar
Juice of 2 lemons

Place all the ingredients except the sugar and lemon juice in a blender in the order listed. Blend to form a smooth batter. Oil a 5½ inch crêpe pan or well seasoned small iron skillet. Add a generous tablespoon of batter to the hot pan. Tilt the pan in all directions to form a paper thin layer. Cook 2 minutes on the first side. Turn and cook 1 minute on the second side. Cook the pancakes over moderately high heat. Sprinkle each crêpe with sugar and lemon juice. Roll crêpes into a cigarette shape and serve immediately.

Apple dumplings

Shortcrust pastry:
1½ cups sifted all purpose flour
¼ teaspoon salt
1 tablespoon sugar
4 tablespoons butter
4 tablespoons margarine
1 egg yolk
2 tablespoons cold water

Filling:
6 large cooking apples, peeled and cored
6 teaspoons sultanas
6 teaspoons brown sugar
3 teaspoons butter

Glaze:
1 egg yolk
2 tablespoons milk

Sift the flour into a bowl. Add the salt and sugar. Cut the butter into small pieces and drop into the bowl. Add the margarine. Blend well using a pastry blender or the fingertips. Stir in the egg yolk and enough water to enable a ball of dough to be formed. Wrap in wax paper and chill 20 minutes before rolling. Place 1 teaspoon of sultanas and sugar and ½ teaspoon of butter in the cavity of each cored apple. Roll the pastry on a lightly floured board and cut 6, 7 inch rounds. Place an apple in the center of each round and pinch the pastry together at the stem end. Place apples on a buttered cookie sheet. Brush each with combined egg yolk and milk. Bake in a 375° oven for 30 minutes until pastry is golden brown.

All Englishmen have nostalgic memories of hot puddings, especially the Steamed lemon pudding, that nobody can make like Grandmother used to.

Plum pudding, recipe page 68, 3rd column

Steamed lemon pudding

6 servings

4 *tablespoons butter*
4 *tablespoons sugar*
3 *eggs, well beaten*
1 *cup sifted all purpose flour*
¼ *teaspoon salt*
½ *teaspoon double acting baking powder*
Grated rind and juice of 1 lemon
4 *tablespoons apricot preserves*
2 *tablespoons water*

Beat together the butter and sugar until light and creamy. Beat in eggs 1 at a time. Fold in flour, salt, baking powder, lemon rind and juice. Place in a buttered 4 cup bowl. Cover the bowl with aluminum foil. Place bowl in a steamer. Steam the pudding over boiling water on top of the stove for 1¼ hours. Heat preserves with the water. Unmold the pudding. Pour apricot sauce over the pudding and serve hot.

Plum pudding

Christmas would simply not be Christmas in England without the highlight of this festive day's meal, the plum pudding.
And yet somehow this triumph of a pudding has got its name from the very ingredient it lacks: plums. It seems that originally plums (or prunes) were in fact used in the pudding, but that at some point they mysteriously gave way to raisins. Anyway, the name does not matter in the slightest, and the plum pudding has been the glory of Christmas for generations.
Probably the most poetic description of the plum pudding that ever flowed from a pen appeared in the 'Illustrated London News' in the year 1848. The delights have never been better described and so we can only quote the passage in its entirety, just as it appeared more than a hundred years ago in the age of Dickens.
'In a household where there are five or six children, the eldest not above ten or eleven, the making of the pudding is indeed an event. It is thought of days, if not weeks before. To be allowed to share in the noble work is a prize for young ambition. Lo! the lid is raised, curiosity stands on tip-toe, eves sparkle with anticipation, little hands are clapped in ecstasy, almost too great to find expression in words. The hour arrives – the moment wished and feared.
And then when it is dished, when all fears are over, when the roast beef has been removed, when the pudding in all the glory of its own splendour shines upon the table, how eager is the anticipation of the near delight! How beautifully it steams! How delicious it smells! How round it is! A kiss is round, the horizon is round, the earth is round, the moon is round, the sun and stars, and all the host of heaven are round. So is plum pudding'.

1 pound whole candied cherries
1 pound raisins
1 pound pitted dates, chopped
4 candied pineapple rings, sliced
¾ cup chopped citron
½ cup chopped candied orange peel
½ cup chopped candied lemon peel
2 cups sifted all purpose flour
½ cup sugar
1 teaspoon salt
1½ teaspoons soda
1¾ teaspoons cinnamon
½ teaspoon cloves
½ teaspoon allspice
3 eggs
1½ cups buttermilk
½ cup oil
¼ cup orange juice
¼ cup brandy
Juice of 1 lemon

Place fruit in a large mixing bowl and sprinkle with ½ cup of the flour. Sift together the remaining flour, sugar, salt, soda and spices. Beat eggs and add buttermilk, oil, orange juice, brandy and lemon juice. Combine with the flour mixture. Pour batter over fruit and mix until all the fruit is coated with batter. Oil pudding molds or empty coffee tins and fill ¾ full. Cover tightly with foil. Place in a steamer, cover and cook 3 to 4 hours or until pudding loses its creamy look. Cool in molds 20 minutes. Wrap in cheesecloth that has been dampened with brandy, or rum. Wrap again in aluminum foil and place in refrigerator to mellow 1 month. When ready to serve, steam 1 hour. Place on a cake stand, decorate with holly and serve with a bowl of Cumberland rum butter, see page 89

Queen of puddings

6 servings

- *2 tablespoons butter*
- *2¼ cups milk*
- *Grated rind of 2 lemons*
- *¼ cup sugar*
- *3 egg yolks*
- *½ cup breadcrumbs, freshly made*
- *½ cup red raspberry preserves*

Meringue:

- *2 egg whites*
- *⅛ teaspoon salt*
- *⅛ teaspoon cream of tartar*
- *½ teaspoon vanilla*
- *½ cup sugar*

Butter an 8 inch pie plate. Place remaining butter, milk, lemon rind and sugar in a saucepan. Heat to simmering point. Remove from the heat and cool to room temperature. Strain the milk and discard lemon rind. Stir in egg yolks and breadcrumbs. Place in the pie dish and bake in a 350° oven for 30 minutes. Spread pudding with raspberry preserves. To prepare the meringue: Beat together egg whites, salt and cream of tartar until soft peaks are formed. Beat in vanilla and ½ cup of sugar gradually. Beat until egg whites are stiff and shiny. Spoon egg whites over pudding. Return pudding to the oven and bake 15 minutes until meringue is lightly browned.

Treacle tart

8 servings

- *½ recipe for pastry for rhubarb pie on page 65*
- *1½ cups golden syrup*
- *2 egg yolks*
- *2 cups bread crumbs, freshly made*
- *Grated rind and juice of 1 lemon*
- *¼ cup castor sugar*

Prepare the pastry as directed for the rhubarb pie. Line a 9 inch pie plate with pastry. Combine syrup, egg yolks, breadcrumbs, lemon rind and juice in a wet bowl. Stir ingredients with a fork until well combined. Fill into the pastry shell. Bake in a 375° oven for 45 minutes until syrup has set. Sprinkle with superfine sugar and return to the oven for 4 minutes.

Eve's pudding

4 servings

- *3 medium sized cooking apples, peeled, cored and sliced*
- *Grated rind of 1 lemon*
- *⅓ cup sugar*
- *7 tablespoons butter, softened*
- *7 tablespoons sugar*
- *2 eggs*
- *1 teaspoon vanilla*
- *¾ cup sifted all purpose flour*

Place apple slices in a 9 inch pie plate. Add lemon rind and ⅓ cup sugar. To prepare the pudding, beat the butter and sugar together until light and creamy. Fold in the eggs and vanilla alternately with the flour. Spoon the mixture over the apples. Bake in a 375° oven for 35 minutes.

Spotted Dick

Steamed pudding with raisins

6 servings

- *1½ cups self-rising flour*
- *1¼ cups freshly made bread crumbs*
- *¾ cup beef suet, chopped into small pieces*
- *10 tablespoons cold water*
- *2 tablespoons golden syrup*
- *½ cup seedless sultanas*
- *¼ cup raisins*
- *2½ tablespoons chopped, candied peel*

Sift the flour into a bowl. Add the breadcrumbs and the suet. Blend the suet into the flour with a pastry blender or fingertips. Stir in only enough water to form the dough into a ball. Roll the dough into an 8 inch square. Spread with syrup and sprinkle with raisins, sultanas and candied peel. Roll as for a Swiss roll. Wrap loosely in foil. Seal the edges tightly but allow room for the pudding to expand. Place pudding in a steamer and steam over boiling water on top of the stove for 3 hours. Serve with butter and a bowl of brown sugar.

Bread and Butter pudding is the favorite of all thrifty housewives because they find a perfect use for old bread.

Bread and butter pudding

6 servings

- 10 *thin slices of white bread, crusts removed*
- 4 *tablespoons butter*
- 1 *cup seedless sultanas or combination of sultanas, currants and mixed candied peel*
- 3 *tablespoons sugar*
- 4 *eggs*
- 2 *egg yolks*
- 2½ *cups milk*
- ⅛ *teaspoon grated nutmeg*
- ½ *teaspoon cinnamon*
- ½ *cup apricot preserves, heated and strained*

Butter the bread. Remove the crusts and cut each slice into 2 triangles. Arrange half of the bread, buttered side up, in a baking dish. Add the sultanas and sugar and cover with remaining pieces of bread. Combine the eggs, egg yolks, milk, nutmeg and cinnamon. Pour over the bread. Bake uncovered in a 350° oven for 35 minutes until bread is lightly browned and the custard has set. Spread pudding with warm apricot preserves. Serve hot or warm.

Apple Fritters are the perfect choice for chilly, autumn days. They taste especially good when they are served piping hot from the kitchen.

Apple fritters

6 servings

- *1 cup all purpose flour*
- *¼ teaspoon salt*
- *2 egg yolks*
- *1 tablespoon butter, melted or 1 tablespoon oil*
- *1 cup cider*
- *2 egg whites*
- *4 small cooking apples, peeled, cored and sliced into ¼ inch slices*
- *2 tablespoons lemon juice*
- *3 tablespoons sugar*
- *1 teaspoon cinnamon*
- *Oil for deep frying*
- *½ cup sifted icing sugar*

Place the flour, salt, egg yolks, butter and cider in a blender. Blend until smooth. Transfer batter to a bowl. Beat the egg whites until they stand in soft peaks. Fold egg whites into the batter. Sprinkle the apple slices with lemon juice, sugar and cinnamon. Dip each slice in batter. Fry in hot deep fat for 6 minutes until apples are tender and the batter is puffed and golden. Drain on paper towels and sprinkle with icing sugar.

Sweet puddings – some like them cold

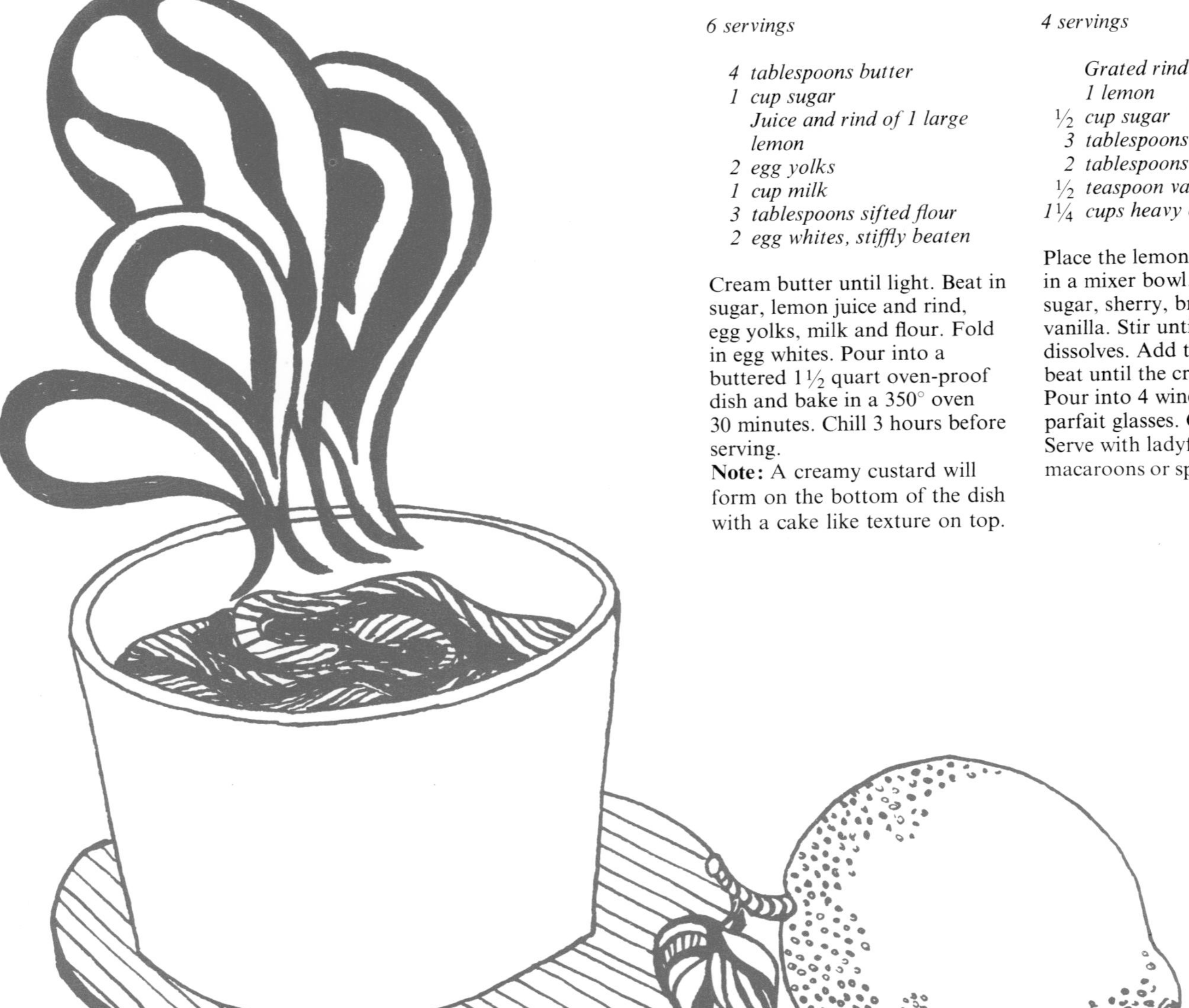

Lemon custard

6 servings

- *4 tablespoons butter*
- *1 cup sugar*
- *Juice and rind of 1 large lemon*
- *2 egg yolks*
- *1 cup milk*
- *3 tablespoons sifted flour*
- *2 egg whites, stiffly beaten*

Cream butter until light. Beat in sugar, lemon juice and rind, egg yolks, milk and flour. Fold in egg whites. Pour into a buttered 1½ quart oven-proof dish and bake in a 350° oven 30 minutes. Chill 3 hours before serving.

Note: A creamy custard will form on the bottom of the dish with a cake like texture on top.

Syllabub

4 servings

- *Grated rind and juice of 1 lemon*
- *½ cup sugar*
- *3 tablespoons sherry*
- *2 tablespoons brandy*
- *½ teaspoon vanilla extract*
- *1¼ cups heavy cream*

Place the lemon rind and juice in a mixer bowl. Stir in the sugar, sherry, brandy and vanilla. Stir until the sugar dissolves. Add the cream and beat until the cream is thick. Pour into 4 wine glasses or parfait glasses. Chill 4 hours. Serve with ladyfingers, macaroons or sponge fingers.

Syllabub

Scottish trifle, recipe page 75, 2nd column

Groset fool, recipe page 74, 1st column

Groset fool

Gooseberry or raspberry cream

4 servings

- *1 pound fresh gooseberries or 1 pound canned gooseberries or 1 quart fresh or frozen raspberries*
- *¼ cup water*
- *½ cup sugar*
- *1¼ cups heavy cream*
- *¼ cup sugar*
- *1 teaspoon vanilla extract*

Place the fresh berries in a saucepan. Add water and ½ cup sugar and cook over low heat until the fruit is soft, (or purée well drained canned or frozen berries in a blender, force through a strainer and add ¼ cup fruit syrup). Force the fresh fruit through a strainer to remove the seeds. Allow puréed fruit to cool. Whip the cream until almost stiff. Beat in the ¼ cup sugar and vanilla and fold the cream into the fruit purée. Chill 4 hours and serve with sugar cookies.

Rice pudding

6 servings

- *½ cup rice*
- *2 cups boiling water*
- *1½ cups milk*
- *½ cup sugar*
- *1 teaspoon vanilla*
- *4 egg yolks*
- *½ cup sugar*
- *1 cup heavy cream, simmering*
- *½ teaspoon cinnamon*

Simmer rice in boiling water for 5 minutes. Drain the rice. Bring milk to simmering point. Stir in sugar and add rice. Cover and cook over low heat for 45 minutes until all the milk has been absorbed. Cool the mixture and stir in vanilla. Combine egg yolks and sugar. Add the cream. Cook mixture in a heavy saucepan over low heat until it has thickened into a custard sauce. Do not allow it to boil. Combine custard with rice. Chill for 4 hours. Sprinkle with cinnamon before serving.

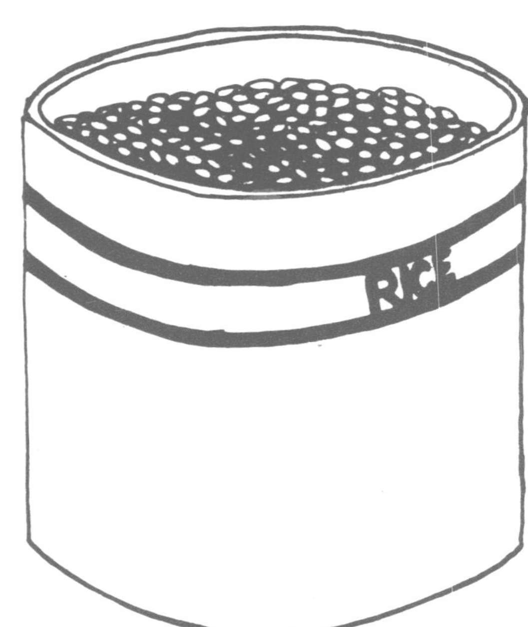

Egg custard

4 servings

5 egg yolks
2 egg whites
½ cup sugar
⅛ teaspoon salt
2 cups milk, simmering
½ cup heavy cream
1 teaspoon vanilla
¼ teaspoon nutmeg

Beat together the egg yolks, egg whites, sugar and salt until thick and creamy. Stir in hot milk and cream. Pour into a heavy saucepan and stir until thickened slightly. Add vanilla. Place in a buttered 1 quart souffle dish or small bowl. Dust with nutmeg. Place bowl in a larger bowl of hot water. Bake in a 325° oven for 1 hour and 10 minutes until custard is firm. Chill 4 hours and serve with fresh fruit.

Scottish trifle

8 servings

Base:
2 (4 ounce) packages ladyfingers, split in half
⅓ cup Drambuie or sherry

Decoration:
½ cup chopped candied peel
8 macaroons (opt.)

Custard:
3 egg yolks
3 tablespoons sugar
3 tablespoons flour
Grated rind of 1 lemon
2 cups milk, simmering
1 teaspoon vanilla

Cream:
1 cup heavy cream
2 tablespoons sugar
1 teaspoon vanilla

Arrange a layer of ladyfingers in an attractive 1 quart serving bowl or soufflé dish. Sprinkle ladyfingers with ½ of the Drambuie or sherry and top with ⅓ of the candied peel. To prepare the custard, stir together the egg yolks and sugar. Stir in the flour and lemon rind. Stir in the simmering milk. Place the mixture in a saucepan and stir over low heat until the custard thickens. Do not allow it to boil. Remove the custard from the heat and add vanilla. Cool the custard for 30 minutes. Spoon half of the custard over the ladyfingers. Arrange another layer of ladyfingers over the custard and sprinkle with remaining Drambuie. Add half remaining peel and all of the remaining custard. Top with a third layer of ladyfingers. Whip the cream lightly. Add sugar and vanilla and continue beating until the cream is stiff. Decorate the trifle with whipped cream and sprinkle with remaining candied peel. Chill 4 hours before serving. Arrange macaroons on the cream.
Note: Strawberry or raspberry preserves may be spread on the ladyfingers as each layer is arranged if you would like the dessert a little sweeter.

Cream crowdie

Toasted oatmeal

6 servings

1 cup oatmeal
1 cup heavy cream
4 tablespoons sugar
1 teaspoon vanilla
2 tablespoons dark Jamaica rum
1 pint fresh raspberries or 1 package frozen raspberries, drained

Spread the oatmeal on a cookie sheet and toast in a 375° oven for 15 to 20 minutes. Shake the pan occasionally to make sure the oatmeal does not burn. Cool the oatmeal. Whip the cream lightly. Add the sugar, vanilla and rum gradually and continue beating until stiff. Fold the oatmeal into the cream, then fold in the raspberries. Chill 4 hours before serving.

Burnt cream

6 servings

2½ cups heavy cream
1 vanilla bean, split or
1 teaspoon vanilla extract
4 egg yolks
¼ cup sugar
½ cup brown sugar

Scald cream with vanilla bean in a heavy pan. Set aside while preparing the custard. Beat the yolks with the ¼ cup sugar until thick. Strain the cream and pour it slowly onto the egg yolks, beating constantly. Add the vanilla extract if the bean was not used. Place the cream in a 1 quart ovenproof dish. Place dish in a larger pan of water and bake in a 300° oven for 1 hour or until set. Chill the cream for several hours. When ready to serve, place the dish in a larger pan and surround with ice cubes. Sift on the brown sugar and place under a very hot grill until the sugar is golden brown. Serve immediately with fresh fruit.

Blackberry and apple pudding

6 servings

- 6 *green cooking apples*
- 2 *(1 pound) cans blackberries, drained*
- 12 *tablespoons sugar*
- ½ *teaspoon cinnamon*
- 6 *tablespoons butter, softened*
- 2 *eggs, well beaten*
- 1 *cup self-rising flour*
- 2 *tablespoons cornflour*

Peel, core and slice the apples thinly. Combine apples with the drained berries, 6 tablespoons sugar and the cinnamon and place in a 1½ quart ovenproof baking dish. Beat together the remaining sugar and butter until fluffy. Beat in the eggs. Sift the flour and cornflour together and add to the butter mixture. Spread over the fruit. Bake in a 375° oven for 35 to 40 minutes. Dust the top of the pudding with icing sugar and serve hot with lightly whipped cream.

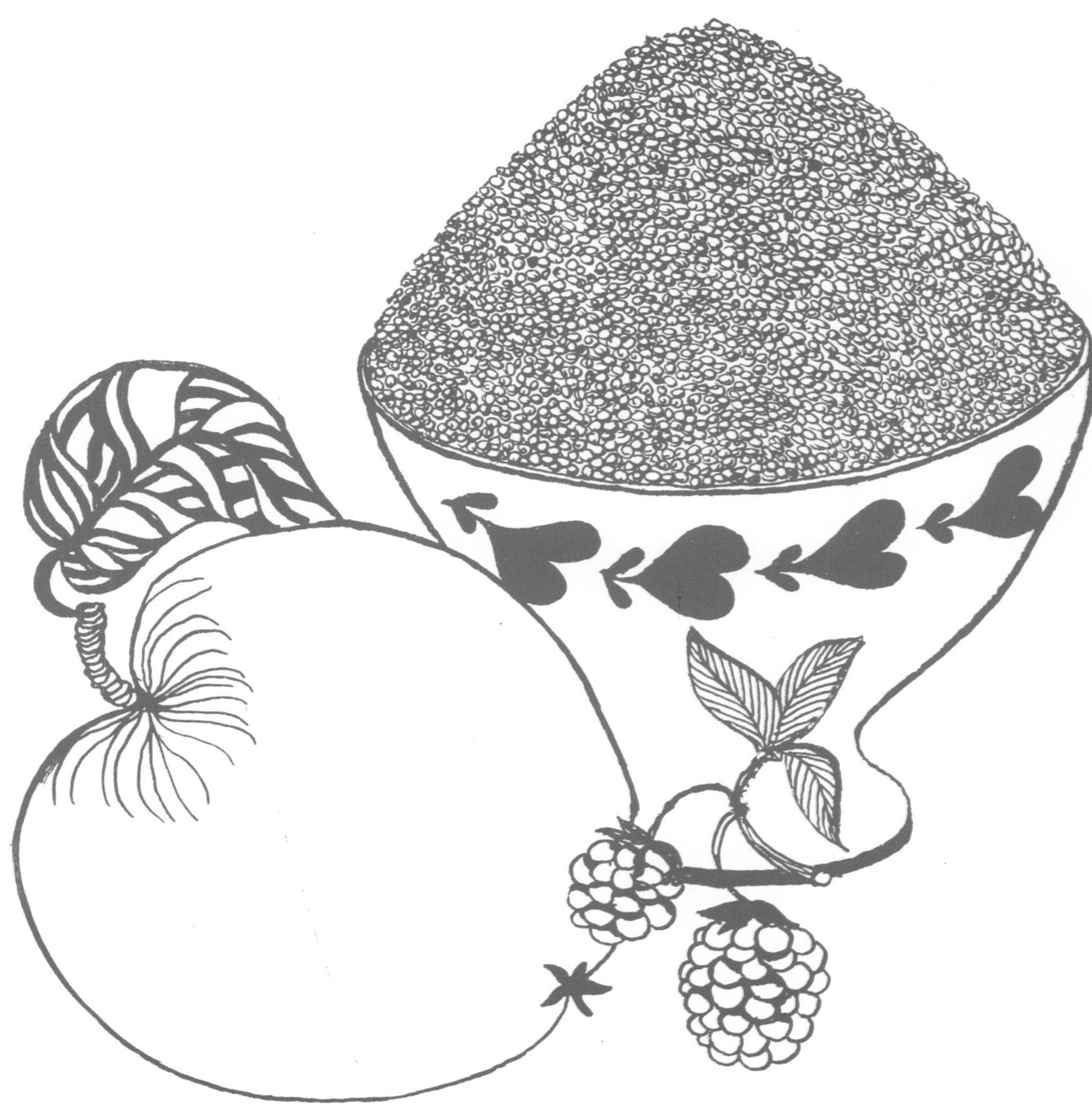

Cakes and scones

Ginger snaps

48–1 inch biscuits

4 tablespoons butter
½ cup brown sugar, firmly packed
3 tablespoons molasses
1 egg
1¾ cups self-rising flour
1 teaspoon baking soda
1½ teaspoons ground ginger

Cream the butter and sugar until light and fluffy. Beat in the molasses and egg. Sift the flour with the soda and ginger and add gradually to the butter/sugar mixture, beating well after each addition. Wrap the dough in wax paper and chill 1 hour. Roll small balls of dough between the hands and place on an oiled baking sheet. Flatten the balls with a spatula. Bake in a 350° oven for 20 minutes. Remove biscuits from the pan and cool on a wire rack. Store in tightly covered jar to retain crispness.

Pitcarthly bannock

½ cup butter
¼ cup sugar
¾ cup sifted all purpose flour
¼ cup rice flour
½ cup ground blanched almonds
⅓ cup ground candied lemon peel

Cream the butter and sugar together until light and fluffy. Beat in the flours, almonds and lemon peel. If the mixture becomes too stiff to beat, knead in the remainder of the ingredients with your hands. Shape the dough into a square or rectangle ¼ inch thick on a piece of parchment paper. Place on a baking sheet and chill the dough 1 hour. Prick all over with a fork and crimp the edges. Mark approximately 1 × 3 inch rectangles in the dough with a sharp knife. Bake in a 300° oven for 1 to 1¼ hours or until golden. Cool and cut into pieces using the marking lines as a guide.

Tea scones

Makes 18

3 cups sifted all purpose flour
2½ teaspoons baking powder
½ cup sugar
½ teaspoon baking soda
1 teaspoon salt
¾ cup butter
¾ cup currants, washed and dried
1 cup buttermilk
¼ cup light cream

In a bowl, combine the flour, baking powder, sugar, soda and salt. With a pastry blender or 2 knives, cut the butter into the flour mixture until it resembles coarse meal. Add the currants. Gradually add the buttermilk and mix until dough clings together. Turn the dough out onto a lightly floured board and pat or roll into a ½ inch thick round. Cut the scones with a 2″ biscuit cutter and place on a buttered baking sheet. Brush the tops with cream. Bake in a 450° oven for 15 minutes. Serve warm.

Singin' Hinnies

Currant cakes

Makes 20 to 24

3¼ cups all purpose flour
½ cup rice flour
1 teaspoon salt
4 tablespoons sugar
2½ teaspoons baking powder
½ cup currants
½ cup cream
¾ cup milk
2 tablespoons melted butter

In a bowl, combine the flours, salt, sugar, baking powder and currants. Mix the remaining ingredients together. Add the liquid to the dry ingredients and blend into a soft dough. Roll the dough out ¼ inch thick on a lightly floured board. Cut into 3 inch rounds and prick each all over with a fork. Bake on a hot oiled griddle or frying pan until well browned. Turn and brown the other side. These are delicious split and toasted or simply buttered and served warm.

Flapjacks

Oatmeal pancakes

Makes 24

1½ cups quick-cooking oatmeal
½ cup flour
3 tablespoons brown sugar
½ teaspoon baking soda
¼ teaspoon salt
1½ cups milk
2 tablespoons melted butter

Combine the oatmeal, flour, sugar, baking soda and salt in a bowl. Stir in the milk and butter. Drop the batter in 3 inch rounds onto a hot oiled griddle or frying pan. When holes appear all over the surface of the flapjacks, turn them to brown the other side. Serve immediately with melted butter and golden syrup.

Welsh cakes

Makes 16 to 20

2 cups flour
1 teaspoon baking powder
1 teaspoon allspice
¼ teaspoon salt
½ cup sugar
¼ cup butter
¼ cup lard or shortening
1 egg
¼ cup milk
⅓ cup currants

Sift the flour, baking powder, allspice, salt and sugar together into a bowl. Cut the butter and lard into the flour using a pastry blender or 2 knives. Stir the egg with the milk. Add the egg mixture to the flour mixture and blend well. Blend in the currants. Gather the dough into a ball. Roll it out on a floured board ¼ inch thick. Cut 2 inch rounds and cook on a very hot oiled griddle or frying pan until well browned. Turn and cook on the other side until brown. Serve warm.

Cooking in Britain is traditional because the people like it that way. And anyone who has tasted the marvellous variety of cakes and 'biscuits' baked according to age-old methods and recipes can only agree with the British way of doing things.
One very old tradition is to bake cakes on a griddle. This is a flat, round, iron plate hung on an iron tripod over the smouldering peat fire that once always burned in farmhouses. A sort of pancake as well as a flat bread made from oatmeal was baked on these plates. In olden days, a Scottish soldier always went to war with a griddle and a sack of oatmeal flour in his pack, so that with a little water and a fire he could bake a nourishing if simple meal anywhere. These traditional griddles can still be found in old cottages in Wales and Scotland.
One of the mainstays of high tea, scones (the name is a corruption of the Gaelic word 'sgonn'), were always baked on griddles and still taste best that way.
The best known Scottish cake is shortbread; it is indispensable at high tea and at such occasions as Christmas and New Year, when it is decorated with sugared almonds and strips of candied orange peels. In the remote Orkney and Shetland Islands, far to the north of the Scottish mainland, the people add caraway seeds to shortbread to make 'Bride's Bonn', so called because it cannot be absent from weddings. In addition to the Christmas cake, there was always a beautiful cake baked with fruits for Epiphany, the Twelfth Day of Christmas. The cake was decorated with colored icing, and a bean or a clove was baked in it. Whoever received the piece of cake containing the bean was king of the feast and was allowed to choose a queen and open the ball.

Christmas cake

Makes 2 cakes

- 1 *pound citron*
- ½ *pound combined candied orange and lemon peel*
- ½ *pound dates*
- ½ *pound candied cherries*
- 3¾ *cups raisins*
- 2¾ *cups currants*
- 1 *pound combined almonds and pecans, coarsely chopped*
- ¾ *cup brandy*
- 1 *pound brown sugar*
- 1 *pound butter, softened*
- 15 *egg yolks, beaten until thick*
- 4 *cups sifted all purpose flour*
- 1 *tablespoon cinnamon*
- 1 *tablespoon cloves*
- 1 *tablespoon allspice*
- 1 *tablespoon nutmeg*
- 1½ *teaspoons mace*
- 15 *egg whites, beaten until stiff*

Chop the citron, orange and lemon peels, dates and cherries. (Reserve a few cherry halves for decoration.) Add the raisins, currants, almonds and pecans. (Reserve a few nut halves for decoration.) Pour on the brandy and let the fruits marinate while preparing the rest of the ingredients. Cream the sugar and butter until light and fluffy. Add the beaten egg yolks gradually, beating constantly. Reserve 1 cup of the flour and sift the remaining 3 cups with the spices. Add the sifted ingredients gradually to the butter mixture, beating well after each addition. Fold in the egg whites carefully. Sprinkle the fruits with the reserved 1 cup of flour and mix well. Fold the fruits into the batter. Oil and line 12 small (5½ × 3 × 2) loaf pans or 2 large round pans with wax paper. Place batter in pans and bake in a 300° oven with pans of hot water on the bottom of the oven, for 1½ hours for the small pans or 2½ hours for the large pans. Cool the cakes and wrap them in cheesecloth that has been soaked in brandy. Place in airtight containers and store until ready to use. Every 3 weeks, redip the cheesecloth wrappers in brandy.

Almond paste:

- 3 *(9 ounce) cans almond paste*

Form 2 cans of the almond paste into a ball. Place on a lightly sugared or floured board and roll into a rectangle ⅛ inch thick. (The width of the rectangle should match the height of the sides of the cake and the length should match the circumference.) Circle the cake with the almond paste and trim the edges to fit perfectly. Roll the remaining paste into a circle the size of the top of the cake. Place the circle on the cake and trim. Let the almond paste dry overnight.

Royal icing:

- 2 *egg whites*
- 1 *tablespoon lemon juice*
- 1 *pound icing sugar*

Beat the egg whites with the lemon juice until they are the consistency of cream. Beat in the sugar a little at a time. Continue beating, scraping the sides of the bowl occasionally, until the icing is smooth and shiny. It will be very stiff. Cover the bowl with a damp cloth if the icing is not to be used immediately. Cover the almond paste with a thin layer of icing. Dip the knife in hot water if the icing is difficult to spread. To decorate the cake, form peaks on the sides and edges of the top of the cake with the remaining icing using the tip of a knife.

Apricot glaze:

- ¼ *cup apricot jam*
- 2 *tablespoons water*

Bring the jam and water to a boil, stirring. Strain into a bowl. Brush the sides and top of the cake with the glaze. Decorate small cakes with reserved cherry halves and nuts.

Irish plum cake

- 1 *cup butter*
- 1 *cup sugar*
- 3 *eggs*
- ½ *teaspoon almond extract*
- 3 *tablespoons golden syrup*
- ¼ *cup finely ground blanched almonds*
- 4 *cups all purpose flour*
- 1 *teaspoon baking soda*
- ¼ *teaspoon salt*
- 1½ *cups milk*
- 2 *cups raisins*
- 2½ *cups currants*
- *Grated rind of 3 oranges*
- *Grated rind of 2 lemons*

Cream the butter with the sugar until light and fluffy. Add the eggs, 1 at a time, beating well after each addition. Beat in the almond extract, syrup and ground almonds. Reserve ½ cup of the flour. Sift the remainder with the baking soda and salt. Add the flour to the butter mixture alternately with the milk, beating well after each addition. Coat the raisins and currants with the reserved ½ cup of flour. Fold them into the batter along with the grated peels. Distribute the batter evenly in a well buttered and floured tube pan. Bake the cake in a 300° oven for 1½ to 1¾ hours. Let it cool in the pan for 45 minutes then remove to a wire rack to cool further.

Chelsea buns

Makes 12 to 14

Bread:
- 1½ *teaspoons dry yeast*
- 1 *tablespoon lukewarm water*
- 1 *teaspoon sugar*
- ¾ *cup lukewarm milk*
- 3 *cups all purpose flour*
- 4 *tablespoons butter*
- ¼ *teaspoon salt*
- 2 *tablespoons sugar*
- 1 *egg, lightly beaten*

Filling:
- 4 *tablespoons butter, softened*
- 4 *tablespoons sugar*
- ¾ *cup mixed chopped candied fruits*

Glaze:
- 4 *tablespoons icing sugar*
- 1 *tablespoon water*

Dissolve the yeast in the lukewarm water. Stir in the 1 teaspoon sugar, the milk and ½ cup flour. Set in a warm place for 20 minutes. Meanwhile, cut the butter into the remaining flour using a pastry blender or 2 knives. Mix in the salt and 2 tablespoons sugar. Add the egg to the yeast mixture. Add the flour to the yeast mixture ½ cup at a time. Knead in the final amount if the dough becomes too stiff to stir. Turn the dough out on a lightly floured board and knead until smooth and elastic. Do not add any additional flour. Shape the dough into a ball and place in an oiled bowl. Cover and let rise until double. Knead the dough a few times on a floured board then roll into a rectangle. Spread the dough with 4 tablespoons butter. Sprinkle on the sugar and the candied fruits. Roll the dough up tightly as for a Swiss roll. Cut into 12 to 14 pieces, and form each piece into a ball. Place "buns" on oiled baking sheets. Cover and let rise 25 minutes. Bake in a 400° oven about 20 minutes. Combine the powdered sugar and water and brush the glaze on the warm buns.

Brandy snaps

Makes 12 to 15

- 4 *tablespoons butter*
- ¼ *cup sugar*
- 3 *tablespoons golden syrup*
- ½ *cup all purpose flour*
- ½ *teaspoon ginger*
- 2 *tablespoons brandy*
- 1 *tablespoon lemon juice*

Filling:
- 1 *cup heavy cream*
- 2 *tablespoons sugar*
- 1 *tablespoon brandy*

In a saucepan, melt the butter with the sugar and syrup. Add the flour and ginger and mix thoroughly. Stir in the brandy and lemon juice. Butter a large cookie sheet very generously. Drop teaspoons of the batter 4 to 5 inches apart onto the cookie sheet. Bake in a 350° oven for 8 to 10 minutes or until golden brown. While the snaps are baking, butter the handle of a wooden spoon. When the snaps are done, turn the oven off and open the door. Leave the snaps in the oven and roll them one at a time into a cylinder shape around the spoon handle. (If you take the cookie sheet out of the oven, the last of the snaps will be too crisp to shape.) Cool on a wire rack. When ready to serve, whip the cream until stiff and flavor with the sugar and brandy. Pipe the cream into the snaps with a pastry bag fitted with a rosette tube and serve.

Yorkshire teacakes

Makes 24

- 1½ *teaspoons dry yeast*
- ¼ *cup lukewarm water*
- ¼ *cup lukewarm milk*
- 2 *tablespoons sugar*
- 1½ *cups flour*
- ¼ *teaspoon salt*
- 2 *tablespoons lard or shortening*

Sprinkle the yeast over the lukewarm water and stir to dissolve. Add the milk and sugar. Sift the flour with the salt into a bowl. Cut in the lard using a pastry blender or 2 knives. Add the flour mixture, ½ cup at a time, to the liquid. Knead in the last bit of flour. Place the dough in an oiled bowl, cover and set in a warm place until double. Turn the dough out onto a floured board and knead a few times. Divide dough into 24 small pieces. Roll each into a small round. Place the rounds on an oiled baking sheet and prick with a fork. Cover and let the rounds rise 30 minutes. Bake in a 400° oven for 12 to 15 minutes.

Richmond maids of honor

Makes 16

Recipe for short crust pastry (page 65)
- ⅔ *cup ground almonds*
- ½ *cup sugar*
- 3 *tablespoons flour*
- 5 *tablespoons heavy cream*
- 1 *egg, beaten*
- *Grated rind of 1 lemon*
- 1 *tablespoon rosewater (optional)*

Line 16 1 inch deep tartlet tins with the pastry. In a small bowl, mix the almonds, sugar and flour. Add the cream, egg, lemon rind and optional rosewater and beat well. Fill the mixture into the pastry shells. Bake the tarts in a 350° oven for 35 minutes or until golden brown.

Drop scones

Makes 20

- 1 *cup all purpose flour*
- ½ *teaspoon baking soda*
- 1 *teaspoon baking powder*
- ¼ *teaspoon cream of tartar*
- 2 *tablespoons sugar*
- 2 *tablespoons butter*
- 1 *egg*
- 1 *tablespoon golden syrup*
- 5 *tablespoons milk*

In a bowl, sift together the flour baking soda, baking powder, cream of tartar and sugar. Cut the butter into the flour using a pastry blender or 2 knives. Beat the egg lightly and add the syrup and milk. Stir the liquid ingredients into the flour mixture. The batter should just drop from a spoon. Let batter stand 15 minutes. Drop the batter from a teaspoon onto a very hot oiled griddle or frying pan. Cook about 3 minutes or until golden brown and turn to brown the other side. Wrap the scones in a clean cloth to keep them soft.

Seed cake

- ¾ *cup butter*
- ¾ *cup sugar*
- 3 *eggs*
- 1 *teaspoon orange flower water (optional)*
- 1½ *cups flour*
- 1½ *teaspoons baking powder*
- ¼ *teaspoon salt*
- 2 *tablespoons caraway seeds*
- *Grated rind of 1 orange*

Cream the butter with the sugar until light and fluffy. Beat in the eggs 1 at a time. Beat in the optional orange flower water. Sift the flour with the baking powder and salt. Add the flour to the butter mixture gradually, beating well after each addition. Fold in the caraway seeds and orange rind. Butter and flour an 8 inch spring form pan or other cake pan with sides at least 1½ inch high. Place a buttered circle of wax paper on the bottom of the pan. Spread the batter evenly in the pan. The batter will be quite thick. Bake the cake in a 350° oven for 45 to 55 minutes or until a cake tester inserted in the center comes out clean. Cool the cake in the pan 5 minutes then turn out on a wire rack to cool completely.

Oatcakes

Makes 16

- 1½ *cups Irish oatmeal*
- ½ *teaspoon salt*
- ½ *teaspoon baking soda*
- 2 *tablespoons melted butter*
- ¼ *to ⅓ cup hot water*
- *Oatmeal for dusting*

Grind the oatmeal, ½ cup at a time, in a blender until fine. Place in a bowl and add the salt and soda. Stir in the butter. Add the water gradually until the dough just sticks together. Sprinkle a board with unground oatmeal and roll out the dough ⅛ inch thick. Cut into 2 inch rounds and place on a baking sheet that has been dusted with oatmeal. Bake in a 350° oven 20 minutes. Leave the cakes in the turned off oven with the door open for 5 minutes. Serve immediately with butter and cheese.

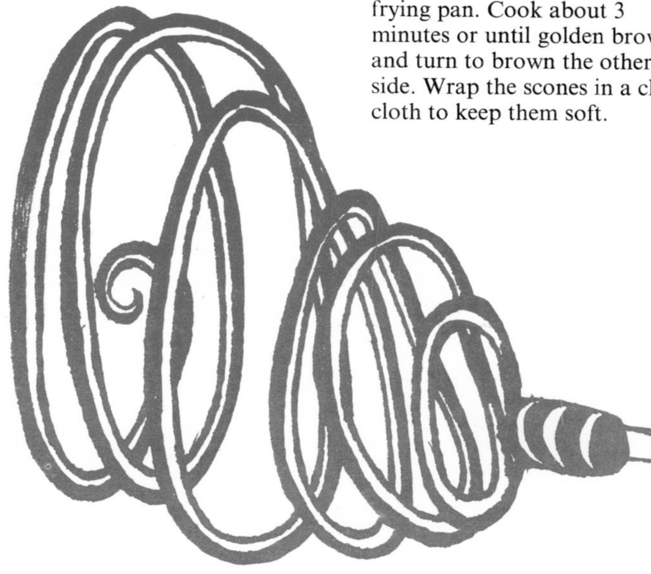

Rice girdle cakes

4 servings

1¼ cups all purpose flour
½ teaspoon salt
1½ teaspoons baking powder
1¼ cups milk
1¼ cups cooked rice
1½ tablespoons melted butter
1 egg, beaten

Sift the flour, salt and baking powder together into a bowl. Add the milk and stir to moisten the flour. Add the remaining ingredients and stir until just combined. Drop tablespoons of the batter on a very hot oiled griddle or frying pan. Cook until holes appear on the surface of the cakes and they are brown. Turn and brown the other side. Serve immediately with melted butter and warm syrup.

Dundee cake

- $\frac{3}{4}$ *cup butter*
- $\frac{3}{4}$ *cup sugar*
- 4 *eggs*
- 2 *cups all purpose flour*
- $1\frac{1}{4}$ *teaspoons baking powder*
- 2 *tablespoons ground almonds*
- $1\frac{1}{4}$ *cup currants*
- 1 *cup raisins*
- $\frac{1}{4}$ *cup candied cherry halves*
- $\frac{1}{3}$ *cup chopped mixed candied orange and lemon peel*
- *Grated rind of 1 lemon*
- *Split blanched almonds*

Cream the butter and sugar together until light and fluffy. Add 2 eggs, 1 at a time beating well after each addition. Sift together the flour and baking powder. Beat in $\frac{1}{2}$ cup of the flour. Add the remaining eggs, 1 at a time, and beat well. Add the remaining flour gradually. Fold in all the other ingredients except the split almonds. Butter and flour an 8″ spring form or other deep cake tin and place a circle of buttered wax paper on the bottom. Transfer the batter to the prepared tin distributing it evenly. Arrange the split almonds in circles over the top of the cake. Bake in a 350° oven for $1\frac{1}{2}$ hours or until a cake tester comes out clean. Cool 5 minutes in the pan before transferring to a wire rack.

Madeira cake

½ cup butter
½ cup sugar
4 eggs
2 cups self-rising flour
Grated rind of 1 lemon
2 tablespoons castor sugar
3 inch piece of candied lemon peel

Cream the butter with the sugar until light and fluffy. Add 2 eggs, 1 at a time, beating well after each addition. Add ½ cup of flour and beat thoroughly. Add the remaining eggs, then the flour and lemon rind. Combine thoroughly. Place the batter in a buttered and floured loaf tin. Bake in a 350° oven for 30 minutes. Sprinkle the sugar on top of the loaf and place the strip of lemon peel in the center. Continue to bake 30 minutes more. This is called Madeira cake because traditionally, it is served with a glass of Madeira.

Irish soda bread

Makes 1 loaf

2 cups all purpose flour
2 tablespoons sugar
1½ teaspoons baking powder
½ teaspoon baking soda
½ teaspoon salt
2 tablespoons butter
¾ cup plus 2 tablespoons buttermilk
½ cup currants

In a bowl, combine the flour, sugar, baking powder, baking soda and salt. Cut the butter into the flour mixture with a pastry blender or 2 knives. Add the buttermilk and mix thoroughly into a soft dough. Add the currants. Knead the dough on a lightly floured board about 3 minutes or until smooth. Form the dough into a 7 inch flat round, and place in a lightly oiled cake tin. Cut a cross about ½ inch deep in the center of the round. Bake in a 375° oven 40 minutes. Cool on a wire rack.

Gingerbread

2 eggs
¾ cup dark brown sugar
¾ cup dark molasses
½ cup butter
1 cup boiling water
2½ cups flour
½ teaspoon baking powder
2 teaspoons baking soda
2 teaspoons ground ginger
1½ teaspoons cinnamon
½ teaspoon nutmeg
½ teaspoon ground cloves
½ cup diced candied ginger

Beat the eggs and sugar together until very thick. Beat in the molasses. Cut the butter into small pieces and let it melt in the water. Sift together the remaining ingredients except the candied ginger. Add the sifted ingredients to the egg mixture alternately with the liquid. Combine thoroughly. Fold in the candied ginger. Pour the batter into a square cake pan and bake in a 400° oven 40 minutes.

Marmalades and jams

Marmalade

Orange marmalade is a gift for which all gourmets must thank the British. But almost no one realizes that this gold-colored delicacy is the product of Scottish thriftiness. On a stormy day early in the 18th century, a Spanish ship loaded with Seville oranges and apples sought shelter in the Scottish harbor of Dundee. The storm raged on, and the fruit threatened to go bad. The enterprising Scotsman, James Keiller saw an opportunity for profit in the cargo and purchased it from the owner for a bargain price. But he soon found to his dismay that no one would buy the bitter oranges and apples he now had on his hands. His goodly wife (thrifty as a Scottish housewife should be) came to the rescue, however, and made pots of jam from the fruit which soon were selling far and wide. This was the first Dundee marmalade, and it has become famous throughout the world. True Scottish orange marmalade must be left to mature in wooden barrels that are seeing service for the third time (another example of Scottish thriftiness). They are actually barrels that have come from Spain, where they had been used for maturing sherry; then distillers make use of them to age Scotch whisky, and only then are the same barrels ready for ripening Dundee marmalade. It is this way that the jam gets its fine and inimitable flavor.

Makes 4 pints

- 2 *large Valencia oranges*
- 2 *large or 3 small lemons*
- 11 *cups water*
- 8 *cups sugar*

Wash fruit well, cut into quarters and remove seeds. Soak fruit 24 hours in the water. Remove fruit and cut pulp and peel into very thin shreds. Return shredded fruit to the soaking water. Bring to a boil and boil 1 hour. Add the sugar and continue to boil until the mixture reaches 220° on a sweet thermometer. Let the marmalade cool 10 minutes then fill into small sterilized jelly glasses and seal.

Mincemeat

½ cup finely chopped suet
½ cup brown sugar, sifted
¾ cup raisins
¾ cup sultanas
⅔ cup mixed, chopped, dried orange and lemon peel
⅓ cup finely chopped almonds
2 small tart cooking apples, peeled, cored and diced
Grated rind and juice of 1 lemon
1 teaspoon grated nutmeg
½ teaspoon cinnamon
1 teaspoon allspice
¼ teaspoon almond flavoring
1 cup brandy

In a large crock, combine all the ingredients except the brandy. Mix thoroughly. Stir in the brandy gradually. Cover the crock and set aside in a cool place for 1 month. Check the mincemeat occasionally and add more brandy, 2 tablespoons at a time, as the fruit absorbs the liquid. After 1 month the mincemeat may be refrigerated if you are not ready to use it. It will keep indefinitely.

Strawberry jam

Makes 4 pints

1 *quart strawberries (not overripe)*
4 *cups sugar*
Juice of ½ lemon

Wash and stem the berries Dry them very well and place in a large, heavy pot. Cut into a few of the berries to release the juice. Cover berries with the sugar and place the pot over low heat. Stir the mixture very gently with a wooden spoon until the mixture becomes juicy. Raise the heat to moderate and cease stirring. When the mixture is a bubbling mass, set a timer for 15 minutes. Do not disturb the mixture from this point other than to scrape the wooden spoon over the bottom of the pan to make sure there is no sticking. After 15 minutes, tilt the pot to see if the liquid on the bottom has a tendency to set. If not, continue to boil a few minutes more. Sprinkle the berries with lemon juice and allow to cool. Stir the berries gently, fill into sterilized jelly glasses and seal.

Cumberland rum butter

½ *cup butter*
1 *cup brown sugar*
3 *tablespoons dark rum*
Pinch of ground nutmeg

Cream the butter with the sugar until light and fluffy. Blend in the rum and nutmeg gradually until the mixture is smooth. Chill until firm. Serve with plum pudding. Recipe for plum pudding see page 68.

Lemon curd

3 *large lemons*
5 *eggs*
1 *cup sugar*
8 *tablespoons butter, melted*

Grate lemon rind into a blender. Squeeze lemons and strain juice into the blender. Add eggs and sugar. Turn on the motor and add hot, melted butter gradually. Place in a heavy saucepan and cook over moderate heat 4 minutes until thickened. Place in 2 small containers. Chill and serve on toast for breakfast.

Toffees and sweets

Treacle toffee

1 pound light brown sugar
½ cup water
5 tablespoons golden syrup
⅛ teaspoon cream of tartar
1 teaspoon vinegar
6 tablespoons butter, cut into 12 pieces

In a saucepan, combine all the ingredients except the butter. Bring to a boil, stirring, and boil about 5 minutes stirring frequently. Add the butter, 1 piece at a time. Continue to cook the mixture, stirring frequently, until it reaches the hard crack stage or 290° on a sweet thermometer. Pour the mixture into a buttered 8 x 8 x 2 inch pan. Before it is completely set, mark into narrow oblongs with a sharp knife. When cold, break the toffee into pieces along the marked lines. Store in an airtight tin.

Hellenburg toffee

2 cups sugar
2 cups golden syrup
Pinch of salt
⅓ cup butter
1 can (14½ oz.) evaporated milk

Combine sugar, syrup and salt in a heavy saucepan. Over medium heat, stir mixture until the sugar is dissolved. Add the butter a small piece at a time. Bring the mixture to a slow boil and add the milk in droplets, stirring constantly. Cook the mixture stirring frequently until it reaches 248° on a sweet thermometer (firm ball stage). Pour toffee into a lightly buttered shallow pan and cool completely. Cut the toffee into small rectangles and wrap each piece in cellophane.

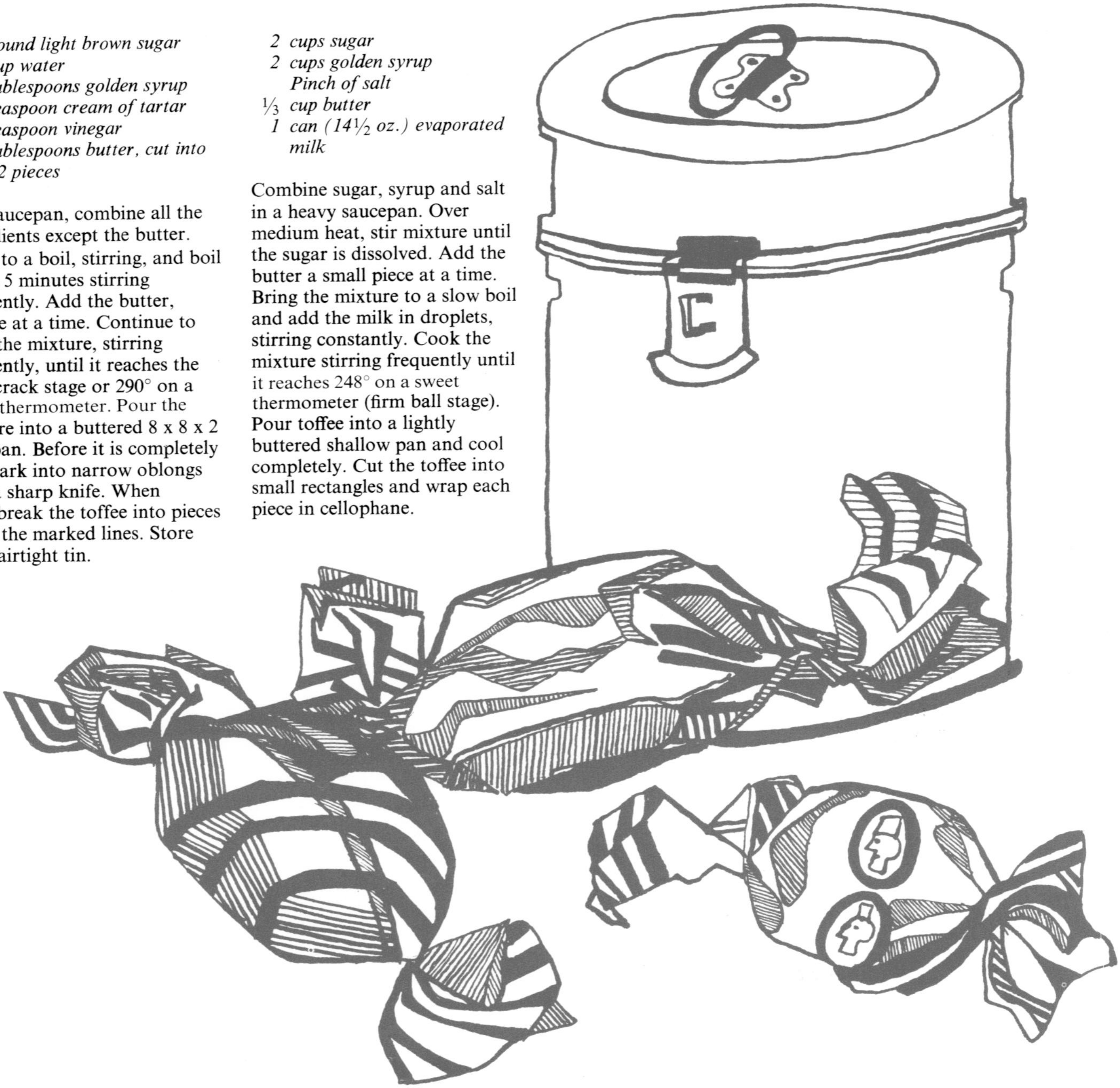

Butterscotch

2 cups sugar
4 tablespoons golden syrup
2 tablespoons cream
2 tablespoons vinegar
½ cup butter

Place all ingredients in a large saucepan. Bring to a boil, stirring. Continue to boil, stirring frequently until mixture reaches the hard crack stage or 290° on a sweet thermometer. Pour onto an oiled baking sheet. When partially cooled mark off into small squares or oblongs. Break into sections when cold. Wrap each piece in wax paper, then in colored tin foil.

Toffee apples

1 pound light brown sugar
½ cup water
2 tablespoons golden syrup
⅛ teaspoon cream of tartar
2 teaspoons vinegar
4 tablespoons butter
8 medium sized apples

In a large saucepan over medium heat, dissolve the sugar in the water, stirring constantly. Add the syrup, cream of tartar and vinegar. Boil 3 minutes, stirring. Add butter a small piece at a time and stir to dissolve. Boil the mixture, stirring occasionally, until it reaches the hard crack stage or 290° on a sweet thermometer. Insert a wooden stick in each apple and dip quickly into the syrup. Place on a well oiled baking tin to cool and harden.

Beverages

Mulled wine

8 servings

- *4 thin orange slices*
- *8 thin lemon slices*
- *8 cloves*
- *3 cinnamon sticks*
- *Pinch of nutmeg*
- *½ cup sugar*
- *¼ cup water*
- *1 bottle red wine*
- *½ cup brandy*

Place orange and lemon slices, cloves, cinnamon sticks, nutmeg, sugar and water in a saucepan. Bring to a simmer, stirring and stir until sugar is dissolved. Add wine and heat almost to a simmer, but do not boil. Stir in brandy. Strain into heated mugs and serve hot.

Rum punch

6 servings

- *¼ cup sugar*
- *1⅓ cups water*
- *1 lemon*
- *4 cloves*
- *Pinch of nutmeg*
- *1 cup rum*

Place the sugar and water in a saucepan. Cut the lemon into thin slices, and add it along with the cloves and nutmeg. Bring to a simmer and stir until sugar is dissolved. Add the rum and heat until mixture is piping hot. Serve immediately in heated mugs.

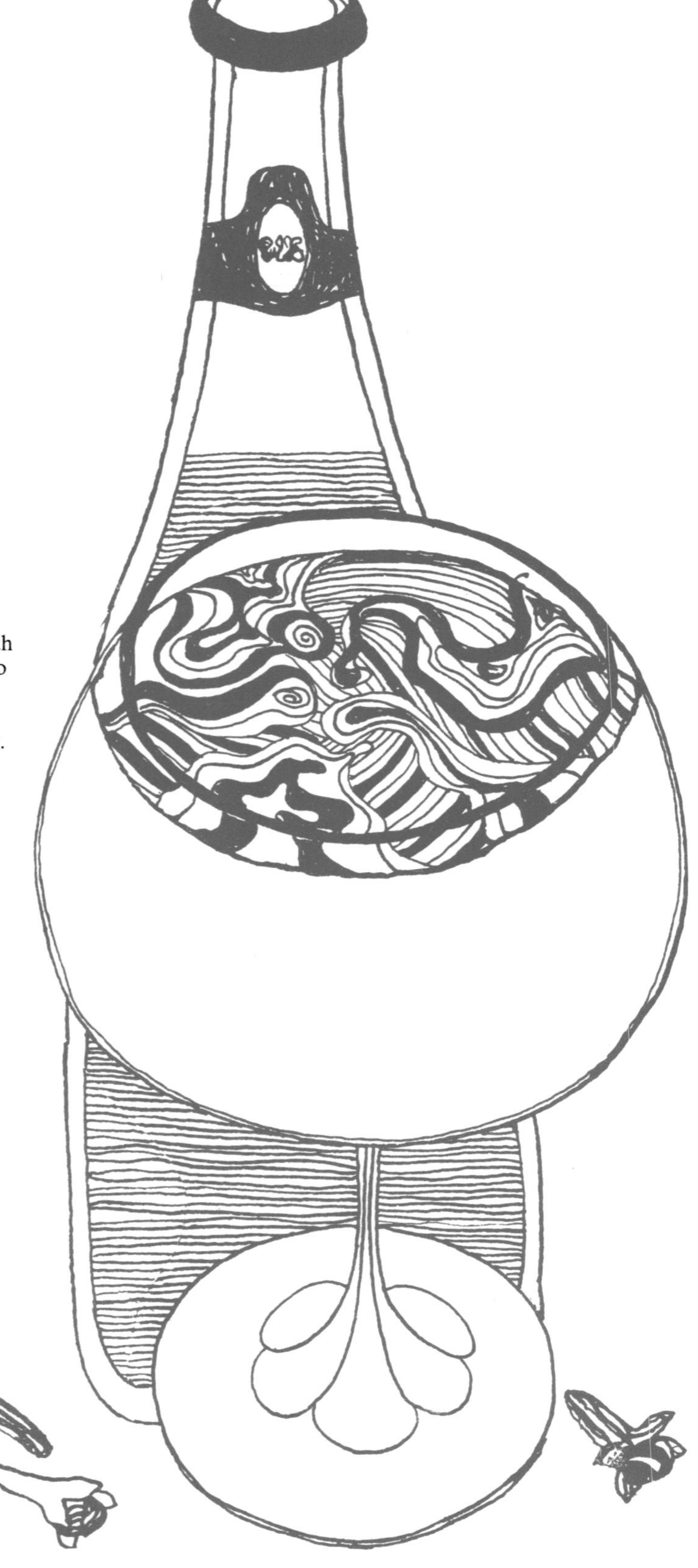

Egg nog

24 servings

6 eggs, separated
1 cup sugar
1 cup heavy cream
2 cups milk
2 cups brandy
½ cup rum
Pinch of salt
⅛ teaspoon cream of tartar
Freshly ground nutmeg

Beat the egg yolks with the sugar until thick and creamy. Add the cream, milk, brandy and rum, beating constantly. Beat the egg whites with the salt and cream of tartar until very stiff. Fold the egg whites carefully into the egg yolk mixture. Place in a chilled punch bowl and dust with freshly ground nutmeg.

Champagne punch

8 servings

4 tablespoons lemon juice
¼ cup sugar
1 lemon, thinly sliced
4 thin orange slices
½ cup shredded pineapple
2 bottles champagne

Combine lemon juice and sugar. Place a block of ice in a punch bowl. Add lemon juice, lemon and orange slices and drained pineapple. Add champagne slowly and serve immediately.

Irish coffee

4 servings

3 cups freshly brewed strong coffee
8 teaspoons castor sugar
6 ounces Irish whiskey
½ cup heavy cream, lightly whipped

Heat 4 Irish coffee glasses or coffee cups by rinsing with very hot water. Fill each glass ¾ full with coffee. Add 2 teaspoons sugar to each glass and stir until dissolved. Add 1½ ounces Irish whiskey to each glass and stir once. Top each serving with some of the whipped cream.

Kitchen terms

Aspic
A stiff gelatine obtained by combining fish or meat bouillon with gelatine powder.

Au gratin
Obtained by covering a dish with a white sauce (usually prepared with grated cheese) and then heating the dish in the oven so that a golden crust forms.

Baste
To moisten meat or other foods while cooking to add flavor and to prevent drying of the surface. The liquid is usually melted fat, meat drippings, fruit juice or sauce.

Blanch (precook)
To preheat in boiling water or steam. (1) Used to inactivate enzymes and shrink food for canning, freezing, and drying. Vegetables are blanched in boiling water or steam, and fruits in boiling fruit juice, syrup, water, or steam. (2) Used to aid in removal of skins from nuts, fruits, and some vegetables.

Blend
To mix thoroughly two or more ingredients.

Bouillon
Brown stock, conveniently made by dissolving a bouillon cube in water.

Broth
Water in which meat, fish or vegetables have been boiled or cooked.

'En papillote'
Meat, fish or vegetables wrapped in grease-proof paper or aluminum foil (usually first sprinkled with oil or butter, herbs and seasonings) and then baked in the oven or grilled over charcoal. Most of the taste and aroma are preserved in this way.

Fold
To combine by using two motions, cutting vertically through the mixture and turning over and over by sliding the implement across the bottom of the mixing bowl with each turn.

Fry
To cook in fat; applied especially (1) to cooking in a small amount of fat, also called sauté or pan-fry; (2) to cooking in a deep layer of fat, also called deep-fat frying.

Marinate
To let food stand in a marinade, usually an oil–acid mixture like French dressing.

Parboil
To boil until partially cooked. The cooking is usually completed by another method.

Poach
To cook in a hot liquid using precautions to retain shape. The temperature used varies with the food.

Reduce
To concentrate the taste and aroma of a particular liquid or food e.g. wine, bouillon, soup, sauce etc. by boiling in a pan with the lid off so that the excess water can evaporate.

Roast
To cook, uncovered, by dry heat. Usually done in an oven, but occasionally in ashes, under coals or on heated stones or metals. The term is usually applied to meats but may refer to other food as potatoes, corn, chestnuts.

Sauté
To brown or cook in a small amount of fat. See Fry.

Simmer
To cook in a liquid just below the boiling point, at temperatures of 185°–210°. Bubbles form slowly and collapse below the surface.

Skim
To take away a layer of fat from soup, sauces, etc.

Stock
The liquid in which meat or fish has been boiled together with herbs and vegetables.

Whip
To beat rapidly to produce expansion, due to incorporation of air as applied to cream, eggs, and gelatin dishes.

Conversion tables

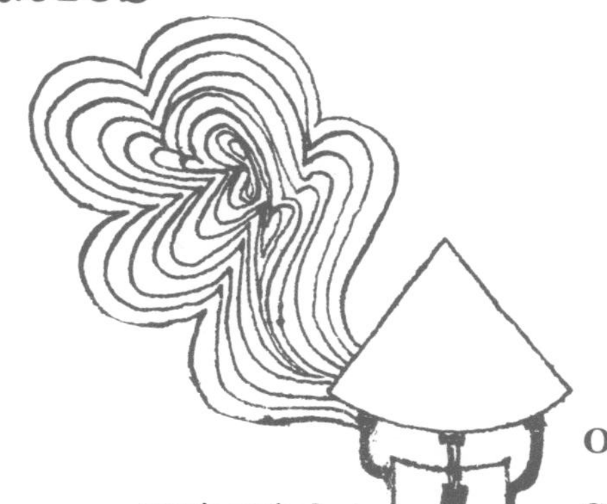

Liquid measures

American standard cup		**metric equivalent** (approximately)
1 cup	= ½ pint = 8 fl. oz.	= 2,37 dl (deciliter)
1 (tbs.) tablespoon	= ½ fl. oz. (fluid ounce)	= 1,5 cl (centiliter)
1 (tsp.) teaspoon	= ⅙ fl. oz.	= 0,5 cl
1 pint	= 16 fl. oz.	= 4,73 dl
1 quart	= 2 pints	= 9,46 dl

British standard cup		**metric equivalent** (approximately)
1 cup	= ½ pint = 10 fl. oz.	= 2,8 dl
1 tbs.	= 0,55 fl. oz.	= 1,77 cl
1 tsp.	= ⅕ fl. oz.	= 0,6 cl
1 pint	= 20 fl. oz.	= 5,7 dl
1 quart	= 2 pints	= 1,1 l (liter)

1 cup = 16 tablespoons
1 tablespoon = 3 teaspoons

1 l (liter) = 10 dl (deciliter) = 100 cl (centiliter)

Oven temperatures

Centigrade	**Fahrenheit**	
up to 105° C	up to 225° F	cool
105–135° C	225–275° F	very slow
135–160° C	275–325° F	slow
175–190° C	350–375° F	moderate
215–230° C	400–450° F	hot
230–260° C	450–500° F	very hot
260° C	500° F	extremely hot

Solid measures

American/British		**metric equivalent** (approximately)
1 lb. (pound)	= 16 oz. (ounces)	= 453 g (gram)
	1 oz.	= 28 g
2.2 lbs.		= 1000 g = 1 kg (kilogram)
	3½ oz.	= 100 g

Alphabetical index

Index by type of dish

Photo contributors and credits

Habitat, Fulham Road;
Tilemart, Pimlico Road;
Merchant Chambler, New Kings Road;
Reject China Shop, Beauchamp Place;
Harvey Nichols, Knightsbridge;
Celtic Design New Halkin Arcade,
Lowndes Square;
Robinson & Cleaver, Regent Street;
The Scotch House, Knightsbridge;
Camera Cuss, New Oxford Street;
Gee Bee Antiques, Brompton Road;
British Tourist Authority,
Covent Garden Authority,
London